Planning
for Your Church

The Pastor's Handbooks

Planning
for Your Church

Douglas Alan Walrath

The Westminster Press
Philadelphia

Copyright © 1984 Douglas Alan Walrath

Book design by Gene Harris

First edition

Published by The Westminster Press®
Philadelphia, Pennsylvania

PRINTED IN THE UNITED STATES OF AMERICA
9 8 7 6 5 4 3 2 1

Library of Congress Cataloging in Publication Data

Walrath, Douglas Alan, 1933–
    Planning for your church.

    (The Pastor's handbooks)
    Includes index.
    1. Church management. I. Title. II. Series.
BV652.W28 1984   254   84-5211
ISBN 0-664-24554-4 (pbk.)

For
SHERRY

Contents

Preface

Why another book on church planning? Because this one focuses on *basic* church planning. Such planning differs substantially from the routine annual planning carried on each year by most of those congregations that do plan.

If you guide your congregation through basic church planning, together you will completely evaluate your church program, as well as the effectiveness of your church's community ministry. You will set overall goals and designs or reshape overall programs. You will plan the basic thrusts of your church for several years. Once you lay such a foundation, I think you will find the annual planning required to maintain and, as necessary, adjust your long-range goals much easier and more effective.

I am deeply grateful to several persons who helped in the writing of this book. C. Scott Planting, my pastor, and Walter Dickhaut, my colleague at Bangor Seminary, read early drafts and offered helpful suggestions. Those who know his work will recognize my debt to Lyle Schaller; he taught me early that church planning must, above all, be practical. Elaine Keenan somehow found extra time to type the final draft. Throughout the days of writing my wife, Sherry, refreshed me often with her vibrant spirit and supported me with her loving care. My daughter-in-law, Kameron, struggled valiantly to type the often cumbersome and unclear early drafts. Then suddenly on a fall

Sunday, her life came to a tragic end in an accident. In ten short months, she gave so much to our home. Her gifts linger on in our lives.

D.A.W.

Advent 1983

Planning
for Your Church

I

Planning in Church— A Practical Approach

Some years ago when I was an eager young researcher, I remember making my very first research report. Actually I recall very little of the contents, but I do remember vividly one significant interruption. I began with what I now know was a much too involved and overly long background explanation. I had made my way through only three or four paragraphs when one of the people present called me up short with the comment, "Don't explain how you did it; just tell us what it means for us!" To say the least, I was knocked off balance by the remark. I hurriedly summarized the rest of my introduction and then gave the group the meat of the report, for which they were—much to my relief—very grateful.

Though many years have passed, I still appreciate what I learned from that significant interruption. Rarely do we need to understand all the theory that explains how something works to make it work to our own advantage. We need some understanding, but we don't need to know everything.

The focus of this book is practice, not theory. It is a guide, not a reference book. If you have begun the book hoping to find a comprehensive explication of church planning theory, you will probably be disappointed. I will explain *some* planning theory, but only what I think is enough to enable you to guide planning effectively in a local congregation.

Indeed, there are certain essential insights you need to keep in mind as you guide planning in a local congregation. Most important of all, the task of planning in a local church is carried on largely by volunteers. In most congregations, only the minister has the program of the church as the primary concern of his or her work life and is paid for carrying that responsibility. All the rest of those who contribute to planning truly contribute; they are volunteers. As such, they are under very little constraint; few if any of them must do what they do. Thus, how effectively they do it, and perhaps even whether they do it at all, depends largely on the kind of treatment they receive from you, their minister.

Your living answer to three questions will go far to determine how well the volunteers in your congregation participate in the process of planning. These questions are:
1. Do you actually want the volunteers in your church to be effective; do you actively encourage them?
2. Do you offer these volunteers real support?
3. Is the leadership style in which you function effective for you and appropriate for your congregation?
Let's look at each in turn. While simple, they are of fundamental importance.

Attitudes

When you work with volunteers in any group (not just in planning) do you generally *welcome* and *encourage* the insights and suggestions of others? Do you want them to be effective? Do you want them to be important? As important as you are?

Probably you have heard the anecdote attributed to various people describing how they discovered that the one secret of accomplishing things is being willing to give others the credit. Often the insight is put as, "It's amazing what you can get done if you don't care who gets the credit!"

Now I know that may sound simplistic or even moralistic, yet, more often than I wish, I watch pastors who are so concerned to shine themselves that they actually discourage the very volunteers they need to carry out their church planning.

Every insight or suggestion offered by a volunteer is a gift. Recognizing the leader and the gift will very likely encourage that person to give again.

Equally important is the way we disagree with others. Ask yourself: Do I usually support other leaders as persons even when I disagree with their ideas?

Some years ago, I made a retreat under the guidance of Gordon Cosby, the now well-known minister of the Church of the Saviour in Washington, D.C. In an effort to help us understand how our need to be right can encourage or discourage lay leaders in our congregations, Cosby shared with those present some insights from an unpublished essay by Carl Rogers. That essay showed us how our tendency to use moralistic language with lay leaders can discourage them.

There is a world of difference, for example, between "That's a bad idea!" (implication: you are bad for thinking that) and "Personally, that suggestion doesn't appeal to me" (implication: you are O.K., even though I don't like your idea). The pastor who needs to be right all or even most of the time is likely to put down not only the ideas of those who disagree but the persons themselves. If he or she does so very often, members are not likely to want to continue volunteering themselves as leaders.

Much of the time, people expect ministers to function as "preachers." In the worship service, they literally cannot talk back to you—and you are supposed to be right. To encourage volunteers to participate freely, you will need to make an obvious switch in attitude when you are out of the pulpit and working with a planning group. You will need to put some distance between the pulpit and your role in guiding planning in order for the other leaders to be able to participate easily.

Another key question is: Are you willing to work *through* your leaders? Will you allow your vision to be tempered by their limits? One of the more intriguing efforts that has occupied me recently is an attempt to understand Jesus' planning strategy. I call it Management Through Disciples. The method is simply this: Jesus obviously has clear goals for his ministry, but he works out those goals *through* the disciples. Their limits and foibles, as well as their gifts and abilities, shape the way in which his program is implemented. He limits what he can do by what they can do. The entire effort is not without its frustration, to which the gospels offer abundant testimony.

His attitude is key to their continued commitment. They know they are essential to him. They know he will work out his dreams through them, not in spite of them. He takes them seriously. He will not abuse them or manipulate them to implement his program. Therefore, it is safe for them to give themselves to the effort.

Church work is unique for the degree of commitment it assumes on the part of those who volunteer. We are asked to give our*selves* to God, and the church is often seen as the place where that giving is acted out preeminently. The minister is often viewed as the one who interprets what that self-giving means. Lay leaders are thus quite vulnerable to abuse by pastors who are not willing to work out their goals for the church through the particular abilities of those leaders in the congregation they serve. A caring attitude toward lay leaders is both ethical and essential to effective church planning.

Support

As a pastor, you can also offer those who volunteer simple and necessary support that will enhance their volunteering.

First, invite caringly. To carry out the tasks of planning, you will need to ask people to fulfill various responsibilities. To invite them caringly is to ask yourself two questions:

1. Does this person want to do these tasks I am asking to be done?
2. Is this person able to do these tasks?

A caring pastor knows the difference between coaxing and arm-twisting. It often takes some coaxing to convince a person to accept responsibility. Many people are naturally shy; others need you to persist in your inviting to be certain that your request is serious and that they are essential. But talking someone into accepting responsibility against his or her better judgment is usually not in the best interest either of the person or of the church. The job done then will usually not be satisfactory, and the cost of completing it will often be too great to the person who has volunteered.

Sometimes a person simply lacks the skill necessary to do the job you have asked him or her to do. Reluctance to accept the task may indicate awareness that needed ability is lacking. Or the person may already be overloaded with responsibility and simply has no more time to take on an additional job. In such instances, *you* have to be sensitive. Some people find it difficult to say no. If you become aware during the process of inviting persons to accept a responsibility that they lack either the skills needed or the time needed, you do them and the church a favor when you share such awareness—and even invite them to turn down your invitation. There will be another time and another responsibility they can accept. And because you have been careful, they will not be tempted to hide when they see you coming.

Second, when working with volunteer leaders, honor time contracts. Once while serving as a synod executive, I asked a very busy insurance broker to head a fund drive for capital improvements at the conference center that synod owns. I really did not think he would accept the responsibility, but I asked him because he was my first choice. I felt that he would do the best job. I remember well our lunch together, to talk over his accepting the responsibility. He probed what the task would involve in considerable detail, almost forcing me to lay out hour by hour what would be involved for him. Fortunately, I was able to do so because at the end of the conversation he looked at me and said, "I can give the time you ask." Also, fortunately, I had estimated the time well, because he held me to the estimate!

Most talented people are very busy. They need to know what your requests will demand of them. They need a realistic estimate of the time involved to know whether they can do what you ask. If you estimate poorly, and the job takes two or three times as long as you said it would, they may complete it, but you may have a difficult time convincing them to accept another responsibility. One good way to estimate how much time a responsibility will take is to go through the various tasks involved with the person you are inviting to do the job and estimate the time together.

Honor meeting times, both beginning and ending times, especially ending times. It is very demoralizing to volunteers to be held in meetings that run long past the published time of adjournment. I have great respect for one pastor friend who routinely refuses to permit meetings to run past the agreed-upon adjournment time if even *one* member of the group objects. If anyone cannot stay past the published hour, the group recesses to meet again at another time. By the way, he has also found that his honoring of the adjournment time has encouraged all members of groups to be present at the agreed-upon convening hour.

Third, ask for feedback regularly. Make it easy for people to tell you how they feel about participating and how they feel about you as a leader. Their feedback will help you to make participating a healthy and enjoyable experience for them. It shows you care about them as persons. One pastor I know provides for feedback by saving the last fifteen minutes of every meeting for what he calls the "check-in time." During check-in time, lay leaders have the opportunity to share their feelings about what the group did during that meeting. They share whatever special frustrations or breakthroughs they have experienced carrying out the particular responsibilities they hold in the church. They share their special concerns for that church. They also share their feelings about the way they or others were dealt with during the course of the evening's meeting. On the occasions when I have been present for this check-in, I have found the sharing very meaningful. The substance of the sharing becomes the substance of the closing prayer for the meeting. People leave with a real sense that they have participated and have been supported as well as having made their contributions.

Leadership Style

Is your leadership style effective and appropriate for your congregation? To be an effective planner, you need to be an effective leader. To help you clarify what that means for you, we will need to work our way carefully through some basic theory.

Many well thought out and substantial books have been written about leadership or management styles. It is likely that you can profit from reading through some of them and will learn some of the important subtleties akin to your leadership style. Yet in my experience, church leadership can be dealt with more simply than most of these books would lead us to believe. Most pastors can function well in a style that is natural to them as long as that style avoids the extremes of authoritarianism on the one hand and permissiveness on the other. The authoritarian leader seeks complete control of the group, while the permissive leader has no control of the group.

Few of us are completely authoritarian or completely permissive in our leadership style—which is fortunate because, except in very rare circumstances, neither of these extremes is effective. However, most of us as we function have a tendency to lean toward one or the other style. Conceptually, I express this tendency in the following simple diagram by describing those who lean toward an authoritarian style as "directive" and those who lean toward a permissive style as "democratic."

Complete control   *No control*

Authoritarian —— Directive —— Mixed — Democratic —— Permissive

◀— Pro-active ——   —— Re-active —▶

What determines your leadership style? Do you customarily say what you think, and advocate it, right at the outset of a discussion? Or do you usually begin discussions with a phrase like "What suggestions do you have to offer?" and offer your own ideas only as the discussion goes along?

First, most of us have a leadership style that is naturally either directive or democratic. If you are a directive leader, you tend to function most of the time pro-actively. Usually you tell a group of people what you think about a particular issue and either gently or forcefully encourage them to follow your leading. If you are sensitive to the suggestions and concerns of others in the group, you also seek them out, encouraging examination of their views as well as yours in the process of leading the group toward a decision.

If you are a democratic leader, you usually begin the discussion of an issue by seeking the viewpoints of others in the group first. You tell them what you think, but only in the process of the discussion, usually offering your suggestions in response to the suggestions of others in the group. You function re-actively.

Second, your leadership style is probably shaped by your denomination's polity. Congregational polities encourage democratic leadership styles, while Presbyterian or Episcopal polities encourage more directive leadership styles. For example, in the United Church of Christ, the minister rarely presides over a board of the church or at meetings of the congregation; someone from the lay leadership is almost always elected as the moderator or chairperson. In my denomination (Reformed Church in America), the minister is by virtue of office the chairperson of the congregation's governing board. The minister is expected to be quite directive in the life of that board, and in most other meetings of the congregation.

Third, your leadership style is probably shaped by what your congregation needs and expects. The senior pastor in a large metropolitan church is usually expected to be quite directive. A part-time pastor in a very small crossroads church in a rural area, where lay leaders customarily carry a great deal of responsibility for the total life and direction of the congregation, is probably not expected to be as directive.

While leadership styles are not right or wrong in and of themselves, they should be suited to the person who employs them and appropriate for the congregation where that person functions. It is important for you to be aware of your leadership style and to lead consistently within it, maximizing the natural strengths of that style and avoiding the abuses that stem from moving toward the extreme beyond that style.

Surprisingly, both authoritarian and permissive leaders manipulate, though we tend to associate manipulation more with the authoritarian leaders because their manipulation is obvious. Authoritarian leaders usually manipulate by overt control of the group. Permissive leaders give the group no direction at all. The group functions like a symphony orchestra without either a conductor or a score.

Perhaps the best way to see how your style is subject to abuse is to consider a bad example of each style. Listen to your feelings as you read through these examples. Ask yourself which of the two comes closer to the way you function under pressure.

Example 1. Within three weeks after her arrival, pastor Ann Zeh decided her church needed to make some basic changes. She called the church board together and read them a very carefully prepared paper outlining the changes exactly as she thought they should happen. It took her an hour to read the paper. At the end of the hour, she asked if anyone had any questions. No one did. She then asked if anyone had an objection to what she proposed. No one did. She then ruled the changes were adopted by consensus.

Example 2. Pastor Ed Adams was installed in his new church only three weeks before he became aware that basic changes were needed. He wasn't sure what to do or how to do it. At the next board meeting he told the members he was uneasy with the organization of the congregation. One member asked him what he thought they should do. He responded that since they were the church's leaders, they should decide what to do. No one talked for a little while, and then one board member said she thought all the trouble started five years ago when the church's constitution was changed to limit the service of board members to two terms. The church then lost the steady guidance of some important older members. Another board member strongly objected to that view, suggesting the church's real problem was its lack of new blood. A heated debate ensued. At the end of an hour and a half, pastor Ed tried to stop the debate with the observation that the hour was growing late. He did manage to convince the board members to adjourn the meeting, but they continued their debate on the sidewalk outside the parish hall.

Rarely does authoritarianism or permissiveness appear in such extreme forms as we see in these two examples. However, if you are a directive leader and things don't go well in a meeting, I'll wager that you tend to move toward authoritarianism. The more pressure you are under, the more you move toward authoritarianism. If you are a democratic leader and things don't go well, I'll wager you tend to move toward permissiveness, hoping that more discussion by more people will resolve the issue.

In either case, you have moved beyond a temperate leadership style, which usually *is* functional in the group, to an extreme style, which usually is *not* functional. When you move into an extreme style of leadership, you make it difficult for other leaders in the group to contribute. They may become so uneasy with your style that they feel the need to protect themselves. If you find yourself often functioning as an extremely authoritarian or permissive leader, I suggest you seek some assessment of yourself as a leader, preferably in a lab setting where you can experience the effect of your leadership style on others. I have participated in such labs myself and found them valuable. In my experience, pastors with extreme leadership styles are not helpful planners in most congregations.

Finally, it is important that you do not have a mixed leadership style. Whether you are a democratic or a directive leader will not by itself determine whether you are effective in your particular congregation. Most congregations can adjust to work well with either a directive or a democratic leader. However, once you have established your style, it is important for you to maintain it. Once people become accustomed to it, they expect to be guided by you consistently within that style.

A pastor with an inconsistent pattern of leadership is very difficult for others to work with. Some years ago, Thomas R. Bennett, while leading a retreat in which I participated, described research that the U.S. Navy carried on with submarine commanders. Crews of submarines live in close quarters for long periods of time. Especially in light of the future nuclear submarine, the Navy was concerned to discover whether certain leadership styles hold up better than others under pressure over long periods of time. Specifically, the Navy wondered whether a directive or a democratic commander could perform better. Actually, what was discovered was that both styles are about equally effective. The commander should develop whatever style is natural.

However, the Navy did find two hazards I think are potential problem areas for pastor-leaders as well. Crews had real difficulty with inconsistent commanders. If the commander was directive in leadership style one day and democratic the next, the crew didn't know what to expect or how to relate. Whatever the style, consistency is vital.

The other set of problems came when the crew expected one style and the leader fit the opposite pattern. When the crew thought they were going to be given a directive commander and were actually given a democratic commander, a difficult period of adjustment followed, and vice versa.

To summarize, identify your natural leadership style; function within it consistently; resist the temptation to move to an extreme under pressure; and, if things don't go well with a new group, find out whether you are the kind of leader they expected. It may take some time for the group to accept your style.

Type of Congregation

The size and style of your congregation help determine the style of planning that will be most effective in that congregation. While every church is unique, I have found that identifiable groups of congregations share certain key characteristics. These common characteristics among churches in each group make it possible to define natural approaches to planning within each type.

From an organizational perspective, I can identify five types of congregations. The key characteristics common to congregations within each type are size, typical church dynamics, relative institutional viability and complexity, organizational roles played by lay and pastoral leaders, typical communication style, and usual planning style.

For planning to be effective, the pastor needs to know how these characteristics shape the planning process in his or her particular church. Some introductory comments may help you clarify which type of church you serve and understand its typical approach to planning.

The very small congregation (usually fewer than 75 resident members) is a tight-knit primary group. Face-to-face interactions predominate; members see one another frequently in and out of church gatherings. The church program is almost always limited to essentials such as worship services, Sunday school, fellowship occasions, and certain traditional special events (e.g., Lenten service, homecoming weekend). Ordinarily the congregation does not have the resources (or usually the desire) to provide a full range of church programs or to support a full-time pastor. However, the church does not feel inadequate because most members derive basic satisfaction from simply being together. The church's being together is its major program.

Lay leaders are accustomed to making do. Except for functions prescribed by polity or traditionally carried on by the minister, these churches are not usually dependent on clergy.

Communication within the congregation is mostly by word of mouth. A few, trusted local persons have most of the authority in the church.

The small congregation reflects many of the same characteristics as the very small congregation. With about 75 to 200 members, it is larger and thus not limited to a core group. It is, however, dominated by a nucleus of members who interact with one another frequently and regularly. However, its active membership includes others who are not in the core. These others know what is happening but don't shape events, even when they hold office in the church. Those in the core group, especially a few "matriarchs" and "patriarchs," remain the guiding force.

The availability of more lay leaders means that the small congregation usually has some program beyond the bare essentials, though that program is usually decided as much or more by the talent available in the willing leaders than by program planning. Thus the same persons offer the same program leadership year after year.

The church's limited size and resources prescribe the roles of clergy to those mandated by polity and requested by local tradition and program. Like the very small congregation, the small congregation is usually not dependent on clergy to carry on and rarely requires or can afford a full-time clergyperson.

Word-of-mouth communication dominates, though print communication is more necessary than in the very small congregation.

The middle-sized congregation (about 200–350 members) can support a full-time pastor and has the human and financial resources necessary to provide a full social and education program. A nucleus of members, often a majority, interact regularly, though most of that interaction is centered around the church building. Organizational activities thus shape the interaction. This congregation is less intertwined with the total social and family life of its members than smaller congregations. Also, a significant number of members restrict their interaction to participation in a church group (e.g., a circle, a baseball team, a youth group, a Sunday school class).

Policy is set formally by the board(s); however, not without the influence of a few respected members (the "pillars"). The pastor is seen more in a professional role here than in smaller congregations. He or she is expected to offer guidance and expertise in most areas of the church life, though laypersons generally dominate in financial matters and building maintenance concerns.

Those within the nucleus consult with one another directly, often as much by telephone as in face-to-face gatherings. Written communication is the norm; print records have more authority than word of mouth.

The moderately large congregation (usually 350–750 members) is a diverse association of groups as well as individuals. One or more of these groups may wish to dominate but rarely expects to do so. The congregation provides programs for different kinds of persons grouped according to age, family type, need, and interest. Many members associate with the congregation through a primary subgroup (e.g., Sunday school class, day-care center, young adult group, senior citizens' program).

Persons elected to boards and committees hold most of the actual as well as organizational authority and power. Longstanding members may attempt to dominate the church's life or direction but are rarely successful.

The pastor is not expected to give guidance in all aspects of the church's life, as is the case in the middle-sized congregation. The pastor(s) and other employed staff are expected to provide substantial aid and direction only in their areas of expertise.

Communication is generally formal and through print, except among leaders within various organizations and boards.

The very large congregation (usually over 750 members) is a comprehensive and complex church with a wide range of programs, staff, and facilities. It attempts, and usually is able to provide, something for everybody—both among its members and for the area it serves. Most members associate with the congregation primarily through a particular program or subgroup that appeals to them. A large number of members are regularly active only within a program or subgroup. No one, including the senior pastor, has current information about all the members. Most staff people know well only those members within subgroups with which they work regularly.

Each staff person is expected to be *very* competent within a specific area of responsibility and expertise. Most major services and programs are directed by staff. Persons elected to boards and agencies hold most actual as well as organizational authority and power.

Communication is largely formal, usually by print, except among the staff and within a formal or informal executive committee, where it is by word of mouth.

The basic approach to planning, both possible and typical, within these different types of congregations varies greatly. Within very small and small congregations, planning is usually spontaneous and informal. Because a few people control almost everything and communication is largely by word of mouth, those who shape the church's life often plan by getting together, talking issues through, and deciding themselves what will be done, how it will be done, and who will do it. They rarely look beyond the group, either for help in planning or for needed data. They assume that most of what they need to know is available within the group. Tradition is very powerful. Because most of what the church does relates directly to the members, and because the members talk freely with one another, such an informal approach to planning is usually quite adequate for much of what the church needs to do.

If you are a pastor in such a very small or small congregation, your most common activity as a planner may be to help church members get in touch with one another better, so they can clarify their needs and develop their resources more effectively to meet those needs. Yet, as we shall see in the next chapter, it is important for even very small congregations to conduct a major review of their life and direction from time to time. This basic planning does need to be carried on systematically and thoroughly. However, such an approach is untypical of most planning in smaller congregations. Members will tend to resist the task, as much because it is out of style as because of its focus. It feels uncomfortable and unnecessary.

Planning is typically more formal when we move to the middle-sized congregation. The church has now grown too large and complex to be governed most of the time spontaneously and informally. For example, the Sunday school is often large enough that it has to be "staffed" each year. Doing so takes planning. Teachers need to be recruited and, one hopes, trained. The same is true with stewardship. The budget will vary as program varies. All members cannot be expected to have firsthand knowledge of the church's needs or feel direct responsibility for its welfare. Both knowledge and a sense of obligation thus need to be communicated through some planned program such as an Every Member Canvass. That, too, takes formal planning and a formal organization. Thus both short-range and long-range planning as well as church organization itself tend to be more formal in the middle-sized congregation.

Formality increases as we move to larger and more complex churches. Typical planning is formal in both the large congregation and the very large congregation. In the former, a defined and regular approach to program planning is desirable; in the latter, it is essential. A large, complex congregation can hardly function without a well-defined approach to planning and without a well-planned organization. When planning and organization are inadequate, leaders don't know how to proceed within their own spheres of action. And they don't know how to interact with other leaders and other organizations within the life of the church. A large congregation that attempts to proceed spontaneously and informally like a small congregation will generally have a disastrous experience. Not only do major reviews of church life need to be planned formally, just about everything needs to be planned formally on a yearly basis.

How formal or informal your approach to planning and organization can be depends greatly on the kind of congregation in which you serve. If you try to impose too much formality on a small congregation, you will meet resistance. If you try to function informally in a large congregation, members will be rightfully uneasy with your style. As you work through the rest of this book, keep the unique requirements and appropriate planning style for your type of church in view. The strategies and tools I suggest are designed to be used in all types of congregations *with appropriate modifications in formality and complexity.* You are the best judge of what will fit your situation.

The Planning Committee

The first question is: Does *your* church need a planning committee? I think every church does. Every congregation needs some group, however small, that has the planning function as its major concern. I use the phrase "planning function" on purpose. I don't believe the planning committee should do all the planning for your congregation; in fact, planning will be stronger if it does not. But I do believe some group needs to be responsible to see that planning happens in your church, and that it happens well.

In smaller congregations, the committee can have as few as three or four members; in very small congregations, even two persons can carry the planning function adequately. In larger and more complex congregations, the committee also needs to be larger and more complex. Twelve is usually the upper limit for a planning committee. Above that number, the committee becomes cumbersome. To meet the needs of more complex congregations, a smaller committee augmented by task forces is usually the best approach.

Regardless of the size of your committee, when you choose its members select them with two criteria in mind: perspective and competence. Consider each of these in turn. Members who view planning from at least four perspectives will help your committee to function effectively.

Program leaders in your church will have to put into practice whatever your plan. Church school teachers, stewardship visitors, and others who carry out the church program tend to view plans from the practical perspective: Will it work? More than any other group, they can save your planning committee from being impractical.

One or more members of your church's board(s) will bring another helpful perspective. Whenever plans involve basic changes, the approval of an appropriate church board is usually required to implement them. Church board members who serve on your planning committee will help you shape each proposal with two important questions in mind: Will the church find this acceptable? and Can we afford it?

You, as pastor, and one other staff person (if you have other staff) should serve on the planning committee. Staff carry administrative responsibility. Even when staff do not personally implement plans, they almost always have major responsibility to see that those plans are carried out. For this reason, staff usually look at what is proposed with the question of Can I manage it?

One or more church members at large, especially those who know the congregation well and are sensitive to the needs and interests of various groups within the congregation, can provide another helpful perspective. Some church members will need to support whatever you plan for it to succeed. So to be on a sound basis, your planning must take the concerns, needs, and interests of church members seriously. At-large members participate with the question Will I or other church members want to be part of it?

Because program leaders implement, church boards approve, staff people follow through, and church members support, at least one person representing each perspective can provide helpful guidance to your planning committee.

Persons who represent various competences also can make valuable contributions as members of your planning committee.

At least one dreamer will be helpful, a person whose vision

is not confined to the church's present reality. Dreamers can encourage the committee to envision *alternative* futures, to stretch beyond present commitments and programs, to consider new challenges.

The committee also needs those who are by inclination practical people. Such persons challenge the dreamers by asking the committee to consider what impact new suggestions will have on your existing church organization and program. And they call the committee's attention to the resources it will take to develop whatever is proposed.

Designers also are helpful. Those who are skilled in building organization can help the committee think through the implementation of various suggestions.

You need at least one member who can guide the workings of your committee. Such a one may also serve as chairperson. He or she coordinates the committee's procedure, keeps it to the agenda, and encourages people to keep moving and stay on target during meetings. Sometimes, especially on special planning retreats, your committee may want to employ a consultant to facilitate these functions.

Someone able to serve as a process observer can also be very helpful. This member's main concern is how committee members fare *as persons.* Do they listen to each other? Are someone's suggestions repeatedly overlooked? Is the committee frustrated and so tired in this meeting that it really should adjourn to another time?

Finally, include some "workers": someone who will keep a clear record of what the committee decides and deal with whatever other paperwork the committee requires; someone to check on such details as the adequacy of the rooms, the presence of supplies like paper and markers, and so forth.

Obviously, some committee members can represent more than one perspective or possess more than one set of competences. Especially if your church is small, your committee does *not* need to have ten or twelve people on it, each representing only one perspective or competence. But you do need somehow to include the range of inputs—and to maintain balance. A committee biased by too many dreamers may never get down to anything practical. A committee composed almost entirely of practical people is not likely to do much envisioning. A committee without any link to the church's board may develop proposals the church cannot afford to implement, and so on. But a committee that combines the basic perspectives and competences just outlined should help planning to be effective in your congregation.

An Overall Approach to Planning

Just as there are two extreme leadership styles, there are two distinct approaches to planning. However, while examples of extreme styles are uncommon among leaders, one distinctive approach to planning is unfortunately very common among churches. Most congregations do only routine annual planning. Even that is more like reaffirmation. They approach planning year after year by taking all their existing program and organizational structure for granted. They rarely ask major, basic questions. They never approach planning completely afresh, with none of the organizational structure or program of the congregation taken for granted. Members of each unit (Sunday school, stewardship committee, and so on) simply review the unit's current activity and then make plans for the future. The amalgamation of various unit plans becomes the congregation's plan. The congregation's overall plan is thus always an extension of its existing commitments and program directions. A church that uses such an approach year after year often becomes hardened in existing patterns. Soon it becomes extremely difficult in such a congregation to establish the validity of *any* new ideas or directions.

In the rest of this book I will describe an alternative approach, designed to provide a base and to complement routine planning.

In this approach, planners encourage *basic* questions—and do so within a setting where persons are discouraged from functioning only within their current organizational roles. Fresh and new ideas are not only accepted but sought. Church-wide or community-wide issues are given most play.

The advantage of basic planning is the fundamental questioning and innovation that it encourages. It is especially useful in congregations that have just relocated or that have recently established new church development fields. I believe all churches need to do this kind of planning. I call this approach *basic planning* to distinguish it from the more confined approach I call *annual planning*.

Overusing basic planning, the same as using only annual planning, carries some hazards. The major hazard to which basic planners are subject is insensitivity to what exists. Their effort challenges the current organization and program. Occasionally, what is valuable in that existing program is too easily overrun and lost. The overall planning program of a church needs to embody the potential gains of both approaches and avoid the hazards implicit in always following one of the two.

How Often Should You Do Basic Planning?

Most congregations can function quite well with basic planning about every five years and annual planning during the intervening years. Most churches already do annual planning in some form or another. And there are many books available to offer guidance to those engaged in this task, some of them much better than others.

Unfortunately, few churches do basic planning well, or even at all. I say "unfortunately" because basic planning lays the necessary groundwork for sound annual planning. It requires you to gather and update certain fundamental data and to make plans that will guide the overall direction and program of your congregation for several years. When basic planning is done well, it builds a sound framework within which to carry on annual planning.

Probably basic planning is rare among congregations because, until recently, few congregations had to do any comprehensive planning at all. Until recent decades, most did not have to cope with any basic change within or around them. They could get by year after year simply by making minor adjustments in their program.

The rapid social change of our time repeatedly undermines many, if not most, churches' programs. In the past century, and especially since the Second World War, there has been substantial and *very* rapid social change. To illustrate, think of just a few contrasts brought about in the last thirty years.

In 1950, four fifths of all U.S. households with children consisted of a working father and a stay-at-home mother. That image of the family is still normative in many (most?) congregations. Yet today, only 16 percent of all U.S. households are "normal" like that! More households today are headed by single persons (24 percent) than by "typical" parents!

Family life itself is very different. There are half as many divorces (49 percent, to be precise) as marriages each year. The number of couples living together who are not married increased tenfold between 1970 and 1980. Over one third of all children now spend some of their growing-up years with one parent. With increasing divorce and remarriage, many other children find themselves with a new parent.

The number of persons aged 25–34 has increased by 1 million each year since 1970, a pattern that will continue until nearly 1990, when there will be 19 million more persons in this age group than there were in 1970. Over 3 million Americans (many of them from this generation) seriously explored an alternative religion (not Christianity or Judaism) during the 1970s. Over 80 million Americans, many of them younger adults or younger middle-aged persons, are currently unchurched.

And lest we overlook harder economic realities, currently we pay three times as much for heating oil as we did before 1973, and $1.35 for the same gallon of gas that cost 35 cents then. The implications for both the church's and pastor's budgets are profound.

The changes are immense; we could catalog them for pages. Regardless of which of them we emphasize, the impact of these accumulated changes is nothing short of cosmic for most congregations. So long as there was only a little change year after year, congregations could get by with annual adjustments of existing programs. Their fundamental approaches remained sound. Continuing rapid social change pulls the rug out from under all of that. Churches wake up to discover that their program is aimed at a world that has disappeared. The old city neighborhood is filled with new people, and the old mainstays of the church have moved out. Suddenly there are only older children or empty nesters (and new grandparents!) in the suburb, along with empty classrooms in the elementary and Sunday school. The farm boy and girl next door return from State U and join their incomes to find an apartment before they get around to seeking the church's blessing on their living together. It's all new, increasing in volume, and challenging every congregation.

Basic planning is designed to put a congregation back in touch with itself and its environment. In these times, almost all churches need to do such planning about every five years. In circumstances where change is very rapid, they need to do it more often; where change is slower, less often. But today *every* congregation—including yours—needs to test the adequacy of its program and organization regularly.

This book will guide you and your planning committee through basic planning. Chapter 2 describes how to go about gathering needed data from your congregation. In Chapter 3, you will learn how to gather essential community data. Unless your congregation is small, I suggest you appoint task forces as described to work simultaneously at each of these once-in-five-years tasks. The two chapters will tell you what kinds of persons are most helpful and provide the methods and tools they will require to complete their work. In Chapter 4, you will learn how to pull the work of your task forces together and shape it into plans. Read the entire book to discover what is involved in the entire process of church planning before you take any steps. Seeing where the entire journey leads will probably save you some false steps.

2

A Church Checkup

Not too many years ago, a city congregation affiliated with a major U.S. denomination fell from two thousand members to complete collapse in a dozen years. Neighboring churches and denominational officials were stunned. Everyone wondered why no one had foreseen the disaster. Yet when I looked through the church's records I could see that its vital signs foretold the tragedy long before it happened. Apparently no one read those vital signs in time—or took seriously what they indicated.

I listened intently several months ago while a veteran pastor described how his congregation had prepared themselves to live with fewer resources. Upon his arrival a decade earlier, he assembled a task force to analyze the congregation's records. He noted a steady decline in this inner-city church. He saw an even more radical decline in the church school over the same period. He then suggested that a task force meet to go through the church membership roll and divide the members into age groups. They discovered, much to their surprise, that 60 percent of the active congregation were sixty years of age or older. The financial secretary, glancing at the list, pointed out that nearly 85 percent of the church's support came from these members.

At their next meeting, the church board appointed a committee to inform the congregation about opportunities to help the church through deferred giving. The trustees designed an attractive endowment fund and publicized it to the congregation. As a result of such foresight, this congregation now receives one third of its support annually from the endowment fund. That support helps the church carry on important ministries to its inner-city neighborhood. They believed their vital signs—and acted. They did basic planning. If your church attends to basic planning, you too can prepare yourselves adequately to meet the challenges in your future.

Basic church planning begins with a congregational checkup. One person coordinates a thorough analysis in which others participate by carrying out specified tasks. The result is a comprehensive picture of the patient—or congregation. The church checkup task force's job is to tell the church planning committee what is healthy, and can continue on as it is, and where changes are needed. The task force provides the committee with a diagnosis of your congregation's current condition.

Over the years in my work as a church executive and consultant, I have helped scores of pastors and lay leaders to complete a church checkup. In this chapter I am going to share the methods and tools I use and have helped others learn to use. By following these suggestions, you will be able to help your own congregation build a solid base on which to plan for the future.

Assemble a Team

The church checkup is best carried out by a team of persons from your congregation. Either you can coordinate the team or a well-informed and well-equipped lay leader can facilitate the analysis of your congregation. If you do not lead the team, I still suggest you serve on it. You will find the actual experience of data-gathering very helpful.

A team effort is stronger because it includes the skills and insights of a variety of persons. Also, when a church checkup is completed by a team, communicating the findings is much easier. While you *might* be able to gather the necessary data by yourself, you would be the only one to have experienced those data, and the burden of communicating their meaning would be yours alone. That places you in the position of having to convince everyone else of the significance of the findings. On the other hand, if you bring together a team to gather, analyze, and decide what is important, the members will be invested with you in the task of helping the congregation as a whole to understand and respond. So a team approach is more likely to produce better data *and* gain more acceptance of those data.

The checkup team need not be large. To begin with, you will need someone familiar with your congregation's records. One or two others who know the church membership well can help to complete such tasks as estimating the age of church members. Another team member should be familiar with church finances past and present. And someone well acquainted with the congregation's history is also helpful. You may want to add one or two others to help with the variety of compilations you will need to make, especially if yours is a church of more than 250 members. In my experience, a team of six persons can do the necessary work.

Call the group a Congregational Checkup Task Force rather than Committee to emphasize both the specific nature of its responsibility and the limited time members will serve. It is usually easier to recruit quality leaders when you clearly define the job you want them to do and ask them to serve for a limited time. While some members of your ongoing planning committee (as defined in the last chapter) may also serve on this task force, unless your pool of available leaders is *very* small, I suggest you do *not* make your planning committee into the task force. It is better to work with a smaller task force and extend the work over a longer period. The planning committee receives the data the task force produces and develops these data into plans (through a process explained in Chapter 4). To shape these data into plans involves a great deal of work. If your planning committee has also functioned as the checkup task force, the members may not have the additional time and energy required to complete the planning process. To conserve their resources, ask others to help.

To do its work, your checkup team will need to have some

instruments and learn how to use them. At the end of this chapter is a questionnaire I have used repeatedly in my work with congregations. By following its suggestions, you can develop a specific instrument to guide your checkup.

One caution: As in a true physical examination, you don't know ahead of time what you will find in your church checkup. Not every question the doctor asks you turns out to be significant. Because you don't know which question will elicit key insights, it *is* important to ask *all* the questions listed. They are well-tested and diagnostic. They may turn up significant data for you.

As you begin to work your way through the questions, you will probably discover that you do not have all the data the questions ask for. Don't be discouraged. You are not alone. Many churches do not have adequate records. Do the best you can. But recognize that you or someone else will probably want to do some basic planning in years ahead, and begin to keep records that will furnish the data you or they will need to use.

Look at Overall Trends

Four key indicators—enrolled membership, weekly attendance at worship, Sunday church school enrollment, and weekly attendance at Sunday church school—provide vital information about your congregation's present condition and forecast its future. Probably average weekly attendance at worship is the most revealing of the four (and, unfortunately, often the one for which information is missing). Enrolled-membership data are usually not as satisfactory because they generally run three to ten years behind reality, especially in a church becoming smaller year by year. You may be able to secure missing data from past years from your denomination's yearbooks or regional office. They may have in their files the annual reports your church lacks. Better and more complete data will strengthen your analysis.

Your church school attendance records also may not be complete. Often Sunday church schools submit only enrollment and not attendance data in their annual reports to the denomination. Average attendance is a *much* better yardstick than enrollment for measuring overall church school vitality. If you can find attendance records even for a few years, use them. As I said before, do the best you can. Research is the art of the possible.

Before we consider what you can learn from these overall trends, let me suggest that you plot your data onto graphs whenever possible so you and your task force can experience them visually. Most people, including me, find it very difficult to appreciate what data mean when they appear as lists of numbers. There *is* a better way. Data on graphs are *much* easier to comprehend than data in tables. Graphs can be photocopied or made into overhead transparencies, even into 35mm slides. When you place your data visually before a group, the implications can be seen much more easily. For help in presenting data graphically, consult any introductory statistics text. *One caution:* to be fair and accurate, you do need to keep the scale the same in every graph when you are comparing similar data.

Once the church checkup task force members have tabled and plotted your data, you are ready to examine your trends. There are some key questions to ask yourselves as you do.

Are our patterns of membership change normal for our congregation? What is "normal" depends on your type of church. Most congregations located in suburbs stepped ahead in all four trends until very recently. The farther their relative location from the city and the newer their housing, the longer their growth pattern persisted. By contrast, most city congregations fell behind, many seriously. Rural churches as a group stayed even, or fell behind slightly. Very recently a few city and country churches have begun to grow, reflecting the growth of population in city neighborhoods and rural areas during the last decade.

The implications of your own trends depend on where your church is located. If you are a city church and have lost members (and church school enrollment) for most of the last twenty years, you are normal. If you are a suburban congregation and did not grow at least in the earlier years of the period, you are not typical. If you are a rural church and your church and church school attendance have stayed about the same size, you are performing at an expected level. (All these trends are from the vantage point of the mid-1980s looking back through the years to the mid-1960s.)

Thus membership loss or lack of growth is much more serious in a suburban congregation than in either a city or a rural congregation. The one clear exception is the Old First type of church, that large mid-city church that is really suburban-based in spite of its midtown location; it attracts its members from throughout a metropolitan region. Severe loss of members in this type of city church is *very* serious, for the same reason that lack of growth is serious in a suburban church. Both require a base of members sufficiently large to support the varied and highly developed program needed to attract and hold faster-paced and often more demanding suburban residents. A suburban (or suburban-based) congregation with its unique constituency thrives insofar as it is able to compete.

Slow attrition of membership is normal for most city congregations. It becomes serious usually only when the *rate* of loss consistently exceeds 3 percent. If you are a city church and your rate of loss has exceeded 3 percent for ten years or more, you need to find out why without delay and reduce that rate. Often the overall cause is a lack of ability to relate to and attract members from the current residents of the church's neighborhood. In my experience, most city churches cannot thrive unless they relate effectively to their immediate neighborhood.

The most serious condition in congregations that have lost a large number of members is overweight. I have consulted with countless congregations that attempt to carry a building sufficient for a church membership several times as large as their current membership. Every strain is more serious in a congregation that has to support excess building.

How can you determine if your church is overweight? If you

spend more than 25 percent of your resources annually to maintain your building, you are probably overweight. When the figure reaches 35 percent or 40 percent, the condition is very serious. If yours is an overweight church, you need to deal with that weight problem in order to free up resources needed for program, mission, and staff.

Reducing the size of your facilities may not be easy. Members of city and rural congregations often live with the illusion that someday their church will recover enough members or church school students to utilize and support its now extra large facilities. Year after year they carry much more building than they need, hoping for a future like the glorious past. Such a future is unlikely. While many rural areas will continue in their current slow growth for the foreseeable future, few will see a recovery of population to match the peak population they had when many church buildings still in use were constructed. City neighborhood churches will find at best a steady but slow influx of persons, among them some likely to be attracted to a city church close by. But membership increases will have to be mammoth to offset the ever-increasing and already high maintenance costs, and especially high energy costs, all churches face in the years ahead. Even the new blood will not carry the excess weight in most cases.

Do you have more building than you now require or are likely to need in the future? Be realistic as you look over your membership and attendance trends to respond to this question. Place your trends on graphs and lay a ruler so it falls midway among the dots. Draw a dotted line for the past ten to fifteen years; then extend that line five years into the future. What do you conclude? If you are building-overweight now and do not see a dramatic growth of members in your future, point out the need to reduce in your report to the planning committee. A church that currently carries more building than it needs is likely to be *much* worse off in the years ahead, especially a church that continues to lose membership.

There are several intercomparisons among the overall trends

that may be helpful for you to complete. Typically, Protestant congregations have an average attendance of about 38 percent of their enrolled members at Sunday morning services. How well do you do? Divide your average attendance by your enrolled membership. If you are seriously behind the national rate (less than 34 percent in attendance), you will probably want to try to find out why—and, especially, whether your rate is falling. One medium-sized congregation I consulted with recently discovered that their participation rate dropped from 38 percent twelve years ago to 30 percent during the past year. Some older members have become alienated as a result of the church's recent new staff and program designed to meet the needs of adolescents. The congregation is now hard at work interpreting the reasons for its new program directions to the alienated older members. If your participation rate is low or dropping, you will probably want to discover the reasons and suggest remedies.

Another statistic that will help you analyze participation is the number of inactive members you have. If inactive members form more than 15 percent, certainly more than 20 percent, of your total members, you will probably want to investigate why. If the number of inactives is sizable, you may need to form a special task force to do the necessary investigating. I suggest that you and your task force categorize the inactive members by asking yourselves questions like: How old are they? When did they join? When did they become inactive? Did issues or personalities alienate them—in other words, did they get angry at someone or something and then drop out? You may discover several groups who became inactive for different reasons. Any significant groupings that become apparent to you will be helpful to point out to your planning committee when they receive the data from your checkup task force.

Compare Gains and Losses

You can gain some helpful insights that may explain membership trends in your church by studying specific factors that contribute to gains and losses. To do so, you will need to gather six statistics for each year for the past dozen years: the number of confirmations (baptisms, if you are of the Baptist tradition and bring persons to full membership through baptism), deaths, transfers in, transfers out, adult professions (conversions), and infant baptisms (see questions 5–10 for details). Generally, I work with the first five of these statistics in three categories and the final one separately. Although you can certainly gain useful information by plotting the data on a graph, in the case of these gain/loss comparisons I find a simple table usually gives me the insight I need to have. What you are looking for in each category are significant *changes* in the rates. How much change occurs and where it occurs provide clues about adjustments you need to make in your church program.

When I work with a congregation, I can usually spot important shifts by comparing the average for the last four years with the average for the previous eight years in each category. You can do the same.

First, compare your internal gains with your internal losses. Internal gains are older children who join your church through confirmation (or profess their faith at baptism); internal losses are persons lost to the church through death.

Second, compare your transfer gains with your transfer losses.

Finally, examine your gains from adult conversions.

You may set up your data as in the following three illustrative tables for St. Matthew's, St. Mark's, and St. Luke's churches. I will run through these examples to illustrate how you can interpret the data from your own church.

St. Matthew's Church is located in an old suburb on the edge of a medium-sized city. It was founded as a new church development field about two decades ago. A comparison of its average yearly gains and losses during the most recent four years with the average changes each year for the previous eight years shows that St. Matthew's is now gaining about five members less *each year* than it was previously. The difference itself (− 5 each year)

GAIN/LOSS COMPARISONS FOR ST. MATTHEW'S CHURCH

	Average for Last 4 Years	Average for Previous 8 Years	Difference
INTERNAL CHANGE			
Confirmations	12	6	
Deaths	$\frac{1}{11}$	$\frac{2}{4}$	+7
Yearly net change			
TRANSFERS			
Members in	27	35	
Members out	$\frac{13}{14}$	$\frac{9}{26}$	−12
Yearly net change			
ADULT CONVERSIONS	3	3	0
TOTAL CHANGES	28	33	−5

is not so great. But the *nature* of the difference does provide some significant suggestions to St. Matthew's leaders. During the most recent four years, the church's confirmations have increased (from 6 to 12 each year) while the death rate has remained about the same. On the other hand, average transfers in have dropped (from 35 each year to 27) while average transfers out have increased (from 9 to 13). Average adult conversions are the same. The most radical change in St. Matthew's pattern is the significantly lower transfer growth—a net of twelve less *each year!*

When I looked through the rest of the church's data (and I could do so because these are data from an actual congregation), I discovered that Sunday school attendance had also fallen radically during the past several years. The church also has quite a large number of persons in the 50–64-year-old age group, much larger than the number aged 35–49. The church building is located on the edge of a medium-sized city in an area that is becoming more and more like the city itself. St. Matthew's leaders had not considered its drop in Sunday school attendance in the light of either its location or the changes in the pattern of its gains and losses when I consulted them.

Combining all these trends suggests some thrusts for St. Matthew's to consider. To maintain itself, this church will need to build its appeal to older *and* younger adults. In light of the age of most of its adults, the church's confirmation rate is probably high only temporarily. Without an influx of new members, once the children now within church families grow up, there will be fewer children to be confirmed. The decreasing Sunday school enrollment also portends a drop in confirmations in the near future. Fewer transfers in is probably the result of less growth in the suburb where the church is located.

We can see what the future will probably be like for St. Matthew's Church by looking at similar indicators for St. Mark's Church, also located in an old suburb, but a suburb that is farther along in the aging process we see beginning in St. Matthew's suburb. St. Mark's Church has nearly twice as many

GAIN/LOSS COMPARISONS FOR ST. MARK'S CHURCH

	Average for Last 4 Years	Average for Previous 8 Years	Difference
INTERNAL CHANGE			
Confirmations	13	21	
Deaths	11	9	
Yearly net change	2	12	−10
TRANSFERS			
Members in	10	12	
Members out	11	16	
Yearly net change	−1	−4	+3
ADULT CONVERSIONS	13	13	0
TOTAL CHANGES	14	21	−7

members as St. Matthew's, yet the average number of confirmations for the past four years is almost the same (13 as compared with 12). However, St. Mark's death rate is significantly greater (10 more a year) throughout the 12-year period; in fact, almost as many persons are now being lost through death as are being gained by confirmation! Also, the drop in confirmations we said was likely to happen soon in St. Matthew's has already occurred in St. Mark's. The overall transfer activity in St. Mark's Church is much less than in St. Matthew's, reflecting the fact that many fewer people are moving in and out of its suburb. Finally, there is a healthy sign, more growth through adult conversions, indicating that St. Mark's Church has shifted some of its energy to attract unchurched adults who live in its community. Almost all its gains are now coming from adult conversion.

Finally, consider some contrasting data from St. Luke's Church, located in a new and growing suburb. This congregation is smaller than either of the other two, yet its current yearly confirmations are equal to theirs. That confirmation rate is likely to move even higher. Why? The rate of transfers in has increased much more than the rate of transfers out, indicating that the church has a healthy capacity to attract those who are moving into its area. This church will do well to monitor its transfer growth. If the rate of transfers in begins to drop (and/or the number of transfers out begins to increase to approximate the number of transfers in), the shift may be an early warning sign. If the suburb is still growing at about the same rate, the church program may be losing its appeal. If growth is slowing in the suburb itself, indicating that the suburb is beginning to age, then the congregation will, in reflection of the community, become more and more like the two churches in the already older suburbs. Changes in the composition of a suburb require appropriate changes in the church's program.

Thinking through your own change patterns in terms of your location may offer helpful suggestions for your congregation too. Rural churches require a strong confirmation rate because they usually lose many of those gained by confirmation when

GAIN/LOSS COMPARISONS FOR ST. LUKE'S CHURCH

	Average for Last 4 Years	Average for Previous 8 Years	Difference
INTERNAL CHANGE			
Confirmations	12	6	
Deaths	1	1	
Yearly net change	11	5	+6
TRANSFERS			
Members in	20	8	
Members out	6	4	
Yearly net change	14	4	+10
ADULT CONVERSIONS	6	4	+2
TOTAL CHANGES	31	13	+18

younger adults leave the community to seek employment. Few of these losses are replaced by transfers in. So growth by conversions and the internal growth from those few families who do remain is very important. When internal growth wanes, and especially if the congregation begins to age, a rural church needs to concentrate very seriously on outreach to the unchurched simply to maintain itself. Fortunately, in the years ahead many rural churches are likely to benefit from such efforts. A growing number of younger adults and younger middle-aged persons are seeking permanent residence in rural areas.

Many of the healthier city churches I have studied recently have a strong adult conversion rate. Such an influx of new adults is essential. Many city churches are losing—or have already lost —the support of their suburban-based members. To maintain themselves, they need to appeal effectively to the growing number of persons from the so-called baby-boom generation who are choosing the city as their permanent place of residence. Many in this generation have little or no history with the organized church. They enter the church through profession of faith for the first time as adults. Some city churches concentrate on ministry that helps persons in this generation to find faith—to the benefit of both those persons and the congregation they join.

As you look at your own gain/loss pattern, consider the interrelation of your congregation, its program, and the community in which you live. Then compare your average gain/loss rates for the last four years with the previous eight years and ask yourself what important changes, if any, are suggested for you by any changes in your rates.

One other barometer *may* provide some clues to your likely future: your infant baptism (dedication) rate. Church planners have known for years that in some circumstances this rate predicts what will happen to the adult participation of a congregation in about three years. No one knows for certain why these two statistics are associated, nor where to expect them to be associated. In my experience, the infant baptism rate predicts the adult participation rate only when the infant baptism rate is *increasing* in a congregation. When the infant baptism rate increases, then about three or four years later the adult participation rate at Sunday morning worship also increases. I suspect one change follows the other because parents who bring their children to the church for baptism (or dedication) begin to participate regularly in the church themselves at the point at which those children begin to participate in the Sunday church school (or about three or four years after their baptism).

So if you are seeing an increase in the number of children baptized each year in your congregation, you should probably make plans for more children in your Sunday church school, especially in the early grades, and more families in your worship services in the near future. If the current increase in the number of children being born in the United States continues (and I think it will), many of us will need to make such plans to prepare for more children and adults in our churches.

Demographic Characteristics

You will gain some very helpful insights if you take the time to classify the members of your congregation by age and family type. If your church records are as incomplete as those in most churches with which I have worked, assembling these data will take some hard work. But the effort is well worth making. In fact, you should gain about as much helpful information from your analysis of the proportion of members in your church who fall into various age groups as you will from any other research your checkup task force carries out.

For purposes of analysis, I usually divide the members of a church into five age groups:

Under 20:   Children and adolescents
20–34:   Young adults
35–49:   Younger middle-aged
50–64:   Older middle-aged
65+:   Senior citizens

I chose these groupings after finding developmental characteristics associated with each of them that are important to consider in church programming.

Those under 20 years of age, because they are children and adolescents, generally require much more of the church than they can contribute. They represent almost entirely a group for which the congregation must provide. Sometimes they do volunteer and make valuable contributions, but even that volunteering usually requires adult supervision.

Persons aged 20–34 are largely consumed by the tasks of becoming established adults. During these years, most of their energy by necessity flows into personal life. They need to establish themselves in work, in separate residences, and sometimes in marriage and in becoming parents. All these tasks require immense amounts of energy and time. The investment demanded limits their capacity to volunteer. When they do volunteer, they tend to function more as helpers than as leaders in the church. Many are at the beginning of their volunteer experience; they lack sufficient background to assume major responsibilities. While almost every congregation has a few exceptional younger adults who have experience as church leaders, most young adults are beginners.

I term those aged 35–49 younger middle-aged. As a group, they are more established and experienced than most younger adults. By the time adults reach their late thirties, the basic shape of their personal lives is usually in place. They are settled in a marriage, established in a home and a job, and their children are of school age. Many have more time and energy to contribute to the tasks of leading in a church, and also enough experience to do it well. Thus, many of the major program leaders in most congregations are drawn from this age group. They represent a group which helps the church "get the job done," whatever that job is.

Those aged 50–64 I call older middle-aged. I often characterize this group by suggesting that those who move past 50 soon discover that they are longer on wisdom and shorter on energy. If they followed the pattern we described for those in their younger middle-aged years, they have gained experience as church leaders. But the process of aging is beginning to take its toll. Older middle-aged persons are less willing to go out night after night to church meetings. As they move through their fifties and into their sixties, they are less and less willing to accept major responsibilities, especially responsibilities they have held previously. They see themselves more and more in the role of giving guidance or direction to the church.

Most of those 65 years of age or older are retired. When people retire from work they also often withdraw from other responsibilities, including some or most of the responsibility they have held in church. Many are still willing to give help and suggestions but do not want to be obligated on a continuing basis. These later years of life are a period when personal concerns consume much energy. As the years progress, many realize they are going to have to do soon whatever they have always wanted to do. Both time and ability have ultimate limits, as does physical capacity; persons in this age group are also more prone to illness.

Once you have divided your congregation into age groups, check to see whether you have a dominant age group among your adult members. To do so, you will need to calculate the percent of adults who fall into each group.

If more than 30 percent of the adults in your congregation fall into one age group, you have a dominant age group. Because people tend to carry their core needs and life attitudes into the church, the mood of your congregation will very likely reflect the mood of your dominant age group. That dominant age group probably shapes the overall mood of your church, the major programs of your church, and even the level of activity your congregation can sustain.

Congregations dominated by younger adults are generally open to innovation. Younger adults are often eager to do something altogether new or attempt something old in a new way. If more than 25 percent of your members are aged 20–34, you can expect your church to try different approaches more easily than churches dominated by older adults. Though if you do strike out in new directions, remember that younger adults have limited leadership experience, financial resources, and time.

Congregations dominated by those aged 35–49 have an excellent capacity to provide program. I consulted with one congregation of 1,200, of whom 47 percent were aged 35–49. Their program, both in terms of quality and quantity, is staggering, and they carried it off with ease. Younger middle-aged persons are eager to accomplish whatever job needs doing. They want to plan, to do, and to build. Congregations dominated by this age group usually have an ample supply of talented, willing leaders.

On the other hand, churches with a shortage of those aged 35–49 have a limited ability to program. I consulted with one congregation with only 14 percent of its membership in this age group. Leaders are exhausted from carrying multiple responsibilities. They exchange jobs each year as though in a frantic game of musical chairs. Most feel too guilty to say no to accepting responsibility, because just about every other leader in their church is already overburdened. If your church lacks members aged 35–49, you will need to be very efficient in your organization and program to make the best use of those leaders you do have—and avoid exhausting them.

Older middle-aged persons (50–64) are generally less willing than young adults to take on new challenges, and not as eager as younger middle-aged persons to begin substantial programs. People in their fifties and early sixties don't want to change things so much as to maintain them. Churches dominated by this age group usually find it easiest to carry out programs along well-established lines.

If your congregation has more than 25 percent of its total members aged 50–64, you may have an oversupply of members with know-how! But unless you also have a large number of members aged 35–49, you may experience some of the frustrations of that congregation with only 14 percent of its members aged 35–49. I worked with one congregation that has over 30 percent of its members in the 50–64-year-old age group. They can design anything, but they were frustrated and the pastors complained about being exhausted much of the time, attempting to carry out the church's program. No one could determine why this church with so much talent was having such difficulty in carrying out its programs. The clue came in identifying the role in which the predominantly older middle-aged lay leaders see themselves. Most of those lay leaders in this church have reached such a high level in their professions that they spend their nine-to-five workdays deciding and referring. They carry that pattern over into their role as church leaders. As a result, the church lacks workers. Those dominant lay leaders unthinkingly transfer their work patterns into their church roles, expecting as church leaders to decide, and then to refer, assuming that someone else will implement what they have decided. I pointed out that their congregation has a surplus of deciders and can't afford to hire the staff necessary to implement all they can decide. What it lacks is doers. Either some of them must shift roles and become doers, or they will have to decide to do less.

If your church has a shortage of members in this older middle-aged group, you probably have an insufficient resource of experienced leaders to draw on and also a shortage of financial support. Often the highest salaries are earned by those aged 50–64; in many churches, they are also among the highest contributors.

As a rule, those aged 65 years or older are least likely to want the church to strike out in completely new directions or begin programs that require substantial investments of time and resources. Churches they dominate are often focused around personal ministry and survival concerns. Older persons often have limited resources; to protect them, they feel the need to live conservatively. Their energy is often limited as well; so large new projects seem even more formidable than they seem to those in their fifties. Older members may oppose new directions, not so much because they disagree with them as because they feel personally unable to take responsibility to see them through. Those in their retirement years often see pastoral care that builds up people and the church as most important, both because they need it and because their time is limited and they are concerned for the future of the church after they have passed on. Out of a similar concern, they also often place great value on programs for children and young people, whom they see as the church of the future.

Obviously, a church with more than 25 percent of its members of retirement age provides real challenges—among them scheduling. Older persons tire more easily. Many have difficulty driving after dark. They fear more for their safety in going out at night. Older persons, as we have already noted, are more subject to illness. They require more pastoral care, not only in times of illness but to help them build the necessary spiritual resources to deal with the crises of loss of loved ones, sickness, and that ultimate crisis—their own death.

On the other hand, older persons do have a great deal to contribute. If your church is dominated by those 65 years of age and older, you may be richer with potential volunteers than you realize! Many churches have not drawn on this richness as well as one city church with which I visited several years ago. Over 50 percent of its members are aged 65 years or older. But this church is far from dead—quite the opposite; the congregation is strong and exciting. Beyond the normal worship and nurture programs, their church functions as a switchboard. They match volunteers with needs identified by individuals and groups throughout their city. As a result, many of their members make important and continuing contributions that enrich the lives of people throughout their city.

Suppose you have two dominant age groups. If you do, then think through the kinds of tensions that would naturally arise between these two groups, as well as ways they can complement each other. Older people, for example, can offer a great deal to children. If your church has a large number of older people and a large number of children, you might think about programming that brings the two together—like family nights, or family cluster education.

If you sense strained relations in your congregation, natural tensions between age groups may be the cause. This past year, I consulted with a congregation that relocated about fifteen years ago. Over one quarter of the congregation are in their fifties and sixties. Most of them still live in the neighborhood where the church building was formerly located. Many are also among the church's largest contributors. The other dominant age group is composed of those in their late thirties and early forties who reside in the church's new neighborhood. Recently, a conflict emerged over a proposed activities center for youth. Those younger middle-aged see the center as absolutely essential; the other group doubts the church can afford it. The two dominant groups have different life views, needs, and concerns. If you have two dominant age groups in your church and are experiencing tension or conflict, divergent views or needs of the different age groups may be a factor.

One final suggestion before you leave the age group analysis of your congregation: Examine how members are distributed within various age groups according to sex. That distribution may give you some clues about appropriate programs. For example, if you appeal to more women than men at the younger adult level, that may be because your program is focused more on children than it is on the needs of adults at that level. If you have fewer women active than you might expect among those in their middle or younger adult years, you may find you do not address the needs of adults (not just men) well. Over the past two decades, I have noted that women who are employed outside their homes (especially women who hold positions of significant responsibility) take on patterns of participation in church similar to those traditionally associated with men. In other words, they drop out when the church does not address their needs directly, and competently, or does not utilize their talents in significant ways. They have less tolerance for busy-work and trivia.

Turning now from age group analysis to analysis of family or household types (question 12), after you have classified your members, make a comprehensive list of your church programs. Note all regular and special events, as well as other services your congregation provides during a typical year. Opposite each household type category, list those programs relating *directly* to the needs and concerns of persons who are in that category. Then ask yourself how closely the program investment of your congregation approximates the distribution of types of members.

Obviously, some programs (like Sunday morning worship) will appear in every category. However, if all or nearly all of your church programs appear opposite every type, your congregation may lack *specific* programs designed to serve those with unique needs, such as single adults and single parents. On the other hand, a lack of programs that appear in all categories indicates the opposite problem. You may need to suggest more programs that include *all* varieties of persons in your congregation.

Your research will be even more instructive if you analyze what proportion of the church budget goes to support services for persons in each category and what proportion of staff time is allocated to serve various types of persons. Many churches discover they spend most of their program money to meet the needs of those who make up a minority of the congregation. I often find such a pattern in congregations that had a large number of children in the past but that today are composed mostly of adults. Yet they still invest the major portion of their education money and staff time to meet the needs of the few children who remain. They invest hardly any funds or staff time to address the spiritual growth needs of the many adults who make up the bulk of the church.

Of course, some programs are simply more expensive to run

than others, and some groups naturally demand more staff time than others for very legitimate reasons (persons going through grief or illness, for example). Still, if you discover significant imbalances as you make these intercomparisons, they may point to neglected areas you should address and/or needed shifts in the allocation of your resources and staff time.

Consider the question about the number of adult members currently divorced (question 13), using a similar approach. Most congregations are surprised to discover the number of resident adult members who are divorced, and they are especially surprised to discover how few of these are presently active in the life of the church. Divorce is a very common experience today; though the rate is beginning to fall, there are still nearly half as many divorces every year as there are marriages. Most people withdraw from the church when they are divorced. My interviews with them in connection with local church consultations indicate that they feel misunderstood and generally unforgiven by the church. If your congregation has even eight or ten persons going through the experience of divorce, remember that for most people divorce is a temporary experience. What you see in the number currently being divorced is a *rate;* you will probably have at least that many in the process of being divorced at any one time. If you have no organized ministry aimed directly at the needs of separating and divorcing persons, you might think of suggesting program development in this area to your planning committee.

Noting the proportion of high school graduates who typically remain in your community (question 14) will give you a rough estimate of the outward mobility for your church membership and perhaps, as well, of the effectiveness of your program for younger adults. If less than half of those who were members of the senior high school class ten years ago are active members of your congregation, do most young people in your community typically go off to college and/or seek employment elsewhere? Or are those young people who graduated ten years ago still residents of your area but not active in your church? If the latter is the case, you may want to recommend that your congregation give more attention to ministry to younger adults.

Estimating what proportion of families live various distances from the church building (question 15) may help you determine how well your congregation relates to its immediate neighborhood and to what extent you need to think about concentrating your church scheduling. Whether the dispersion of the congregation is of significant concern depends on the type of neighborhood around your church building. We shall address this issue in depth in the next chapter. At this point, we simply need to note that a widely scattered congregation in a rural area whose members drive some distance to the church building may need to deal with the issue of scheduling but probably not with the issue of social distance between current members and current neighborhood residents. Probably those active in the church are similar to those who reside in the area.

On the other hand, a city church with a congregation composed of members who formerly lived in the neighborhood around the building but who moved out as the neighborhood changed, and whose neighborhood now is composed of persons socially and/or economically different from the church membership, not only has a scheduling problem but a mission issue to face. It is out of touch with its immediate neighborhood. The distance between the church and the neighborhood is social and cultural as well as geographical.

Generally speaking, I have found that people will drive five to seven miles or from twenty to twenty-five minutes before they begin to complain seriously about the inconvenience of travel between their place of residence and the church building. Thus, if a large proportion of your congregation lives five or more miles away, you may need to consider clustering your church events, if you do not already do so. Such clustering, which is more convenient for those who must travel long distances to attend, may increase the level of participation in your church program.

Financial Analysis

Surprisingly, most people have difficulty comprehending the significance of church financial reports, especially such year-by-year comparisons as you will find in questions 16–22. Before you begin to work up your own church's financial data, let me offer two suggestions I have found helpful when completing and sharing analyses of church finances. First, always provide frames of reference that help point up the significance of your data; second, whenever possible, present your data graphically as well as in tables.

We have already noted the importance of graphic presentation. To illustrate the need for adequate frames of reference, consider the table for St. John's Church, which contains actual numbers from a congregation with whom I consulted recently. Reading down the first column under Receipts, you might conclude that this congregation has enjoyed a fairly healthy increase in its stewardship over the last decade and that its current financial condition is much better than that of ten years ago. But look closely at the second column. This column converts the ten-year receipts to constant dollars: Every dollar in the final year, 1982, has the same purchasing power as every dollar ten years previously.

Actually, this congregation is barely keeping up with inflation and for the past two years has begun to run behind. You can see this clearly only because the second column converts the receipts into 1967 dollars (by multiplying the dollars that were contributed during each year by what those dollars were actually worth in terms of 1967 dollars). Thus, each dollar of the $176,298 contributed in 1982 was worth only .344 cents, or a total of $60,647. Contributions for this church were actually higher in 1973 than in 1982, when expressed in constant dollars. In 1973, of the $90,739 contributed, each dollar was worth .752 cents, for a total of $68,236, which is $7,589 more real income than the church received ten years later.

The factors you need to employ to correct the receipts from your congregation for any given set of years are readily obtainable from the Bureau of Labor Statistics, U.S. Department of Labor. They appear in a wide variety of publications (for example, *The World Almanac and Book of Facts* published annually by the Newspaper Enterprise Association).

ST. JOHN'S CHURCH
TEN-YEAR COMPARISON OF RECEIPTS

Year	*Receipts*	
	Current $	*Constant (1967) $*
1973	90,739	68,236 (.752)
1974	90,630	61,357 (.677)
1975	105,742	65,560 (.620)
1976	107,058	62,843 (.587)
1977	125,864	69,351 (.551)
1978	124,556	61,406 (.493)
1979	116,643	53,772 (.461)
1980	170,236	69,116 (.406)
1981	173,438	63,652 (.367)
1982	176,298	60,647 (.344)

The use of adequate frames of reference will help you and your task force to see what your real trends are. Make the comparisons not only for your total church income but for each category listed in questions 17–20. You will see readily not only whether you are really keeping up but whether your support base is shifting. Such shifts are important to monitor. If your income is moving upward in one category (e.g., receipts from living donors) and downward in another (e.g., endowment income or income from church organizations), that trend may hold significant consequences for your church.

Many churches, for example, have depended for years on money raised by one or two key organizations to provide a substantial portion of their support. But organizations dwindle in size, sometimes their members age, or the events they have conducted lose their popularity. Income lost or likely to be lost in one category thus needs to be made up in another, if even the same level of support is to be maintained. As you analyze the various trends, on the basis of the direction in which you are now headed, what do you see in the future? What changes need to be explored? And, of course, don't forget to plot on graphs any significant trends you want to call to the attention of the planning committee, along with clarifying frames of reference.

In addition to helping you discover whether your congregation is keeping up with inflation, the various financial statistics suggested in Part IV of the questionnaire will help you to analyze your church givers. Many congregations depend on a very small number of members for a great deal of their support. Recently, I consulted with a congregation that listed 210 giving units of record (a giving unit of record is either an individual or a household who contribute to the church regularly, regardless of whether an actual pledge to the church is made). The average unit in this congregation contributed $1,317 in 1982 (obtained by dividing the total contributions from member giving—$276,-500—by the total number of giving units). An average gift of $25.33 weekly (obtained by dividing the annual average of $1,-317 by 52 weeks) appears to be quite healthy.

However, the ten units that contributed the most money in 1982 together contributed $80,263, which represents 29 percent of the money received from members in that year. The next ten largest giving units contributed $47,000, which represents an additional 17 percent of the money received from member giving in 1982. Combining the two, I discovered that this congregation actually receives 46 percent of its contributions, or almost half, from less than 10 percent of its 210 giving units! I then went on with my analysis. I took the $276,500 contributed from members and subtracted the $127,263 given by those first 20 units. I then produced a clarifying frame of reference by dividing the *remaining* contributors' gifts ($149,237) by the *remaining* giving units (190). Thus, the "typical" unit contributed about $785 last year, not nearly so impressive.

But there is still more to consider. The congregation actually has over 400 resident households—about 420. Thus, only half the households contribute regularly to the church's support. If we again remove those 20 untypical units and their contributions, and then divide the $149,237 given last year by the remaining 400 households, the result is a modest average household contribution of only $373 to the church, or about a dollar a day.

Analyze the member giving of your own congregation to determine whether your support base is dangerously concentrated in a few givers. If more than 20 percent of your member giving is contributed by the first or highest 20 units, what significance has that for you currently and in the future? For example, how old are the persons represented in these units? In one congregation, when the financial secretary furnished me with a list of ages of the twenty highest contributors, they were *all* sixty years of age or older! How much power or influence do those who give the most exert in the church (whether they actually seek that influence or not)?

Finally, you will probably find it helpful to consider in some depth how much of your support comes from various categories of support (questions 17–20) and whether there are changes in any categories to which you want or need to call attention. Asking such questions had a profound impact on the congregation whose story we noted at the beginning of this chapter. When they realized the advancing age of the majority of their members, they decided that the development of an endowment fund was the only way to ensure that they could continue their important ministry as an inner-city church.

They are very much with the times in their assumptions. When I began to work as a pastor nearly three decades ago, most planners believed that a church *with* an endowment of any real size would be likely to experience financial difficulty. Their logic ran that church members, aware of the large endowment, would not contribute substantially to the support of the church. Such was often the case in those days, and it still is in some instances.

However, in more congregations today the reverse is true. Many congregations are likely to experience financial difficulty if they do *not* have substantial endowments, especially churches in changing (or changed) city neighborhoods that find they can continue vital ministries in the neighborhoods only if they can find ways to perpetuate income from their dwindling middle-class constituencies. The neighborhood people often need ministries but cannot afford themselves to support the congregation that provides them. An endowment is one way to ensure that the ministry will continue.

Income from rents or service fees is another. When energy was relatively cheap and typical church memberships were sizable, congregations could give the use of their buildings to various groups with little consideration of the added expense such free use involved. Many of these same congregations can no longer afford to be quite so liberal.

If you make your church building available to outside groups, or to nonmembers for such purposes as weddings, you may want to recommend at least informing those who use the building of the added cost of such use. Though your church may not want to discourage outsiders from using the building by charging a fee, you may want to encourage a "share the burden of support" policy— especially with groups that can afford to pay and are focused on neither charitable nor church-related concerns.

Pulling It All Together

At the same time at which your task force is collecting data on the items we have considered so far in this chapter, ask various program units (or, if you are a smaller congregation, persons responsible to conduct program in your congregation) to write answers to four questions:

1. What program or ministry does your unit (do you) do best?
2. What programs or ministries has your unit (have you) terminated during the past five years?
3. What program or ministry do you think your unit needs (you need) most to develop during the next five years?
4. What do you see as the two or three most significant issues before this congregation today?

When you have assembled all the other data required for your church checkup and have outlined the implications of those data for your congregation, consider these implications in light of the answers the program units (or persons) give to the four questions listed above. Within your congregational checkup task force, discuss carefully which units (or persons) seem to be aware of which of the issues or problems you have identified. Have they raised issues you overlooked? If their issues seem significant, don't hesitate to point them up in your report. Has your analysis identified issues of which no one outside your task force seems to be aware? If so, you will have to point up well the significance of these issues.

When you compose your report to the planning committee, the concerns you raise will probably elicit a stronger response if you:

1. Summarize your recommendations at the beginning.
2. Suggest specific referrals to existing persons or units wherever possible.
3. Provide supporting evidence in detail in an appendix.

Where your task force data agree with suggested concerns and recommendations offered by program units (or persons), praise the units for their perceptiveness. Where the data you have gathered indicate that units need to give attention to concerns they do not mention, be certain to marshal sound support especially for these recommendations. Finally, where your data point up areas of concern that are new, describe these clearly and again offer supporting evidence.

Be sure to share your sense of priority as a task force with the planning committee in your report. Focus their attention. Reading through the description of how the planning committee will use your report in Chapter 4 will also provide helpful suggestions to guide your preparation (see especially the first two sections).

A CHURCH CHECKUP QUESTIONNAIRE*

Part I: Membership Enrollment and Attendance Trends

1. What was the *total membership* of your congregation in each of the years listed? (Place an asterisk [*] next to years when changes reflect significant roll revisions.)

25 years ago____	19____	13____	7____
23 years ago____	17____	11____	5____
21 years ago____	15____	9____	3____
			Last year ____

How many *inactive members* are included in last year's figure?____

*Many of these questions are based on suggestions given to me some years ago by Lyle Schaller.

Repeat this list of years for questions 2–4.

2. What was your average *attendance at morning services* in each of the years listed? (If your major weekly service is at some time other than Sunday morning, use attendance figures for this service.)

3. What was your total *enrollment in Sunday church school* (adults and children) in each of the years listed?

4. What was your average *attendance at Sunday church school* (adults and children) in each of the years listed?

Part II: Gains and Losses

5. How many members did you receive by *confirmation* (or baptism, as young people) in each of the years listed?

12 years ago____	9____	6____	3____
11 years ago____	8____	5____	2____
			Last
10 years ago____	7____	4____	year____

Repeat this list of years for questions 6–10.

6. How many *deaths* of church members occurred in each of the years listed?

7. How many persons *transferred in* by letter in each of the years listed?

8. How many persons *transferred out* by letter in each of the years listed?

9. How many *new members* were received by profession of faith as *adults* in each of the years listed?

10. How many infants or small children were *baptized* (dedicated, christened) in each of the years listed?

Part III: Demographic Characteristics

11. List the number of male and female resident members who
    fall in each of the following age groups:

Males	*Females*	*All*	*Percent*
Under 20_____	Under 20_____	Under 20_____	_____
20–34_____	20–34_____	20–34_____	_____
35–49_____	35–49_____	35–49_____	_____
50–64_____	50–64_____	50–64_____	_____
65+_____	65+_____	65+_____	_____
Total_____	Total_____	Total_____	_____

12. List the number and percent of resident adult members (age
    20 and over) in each of the following categories:

Number   *Percent*

_____   _____   Husbands and wives living together with chil-
                  dren under 20 at home*

_____   _____   Husbands and wives living together *without*
                  children under 20 at home*

_____   _____   Single adults, including never married, sepa-
                  rated, and divorced

_____   _____   Widows and widowers

_____   _____   One-parent households with children under
                  20 at home

_____   _____   Others (describe)_____

_____   _____   Total

13. List the number of resident adult members who are cur-
    rently: Separated_____ Divorced_____

14. What percentage of those who were seniors in high school
    and members of your church ten years ago are still members
    of your congregation today? (Check one)

---

*If only one spouse is a member, count the *member* in the appropriate
category.

_____Fewer than 25%_____25%–49%_____50%–74%
_____75% or more

15. How many church families live each of the following distances (in miles) from your church building?

Less than ½_____ 1–2_____3–5_____ 10–25_____
      ½–1_____2–3_____5–10_____over 25_____

Part IV: Financial Data

16. What were the *total receipts* of your church during each of the years listed?

12 years ago $_____ 9 $_____ 6 $_____   3 $_____
11 years ago $_____ 8 $_____ 5 $_____   2 $_____
                                          Last
10 years ago $_____ 7 $_____ 4 $_____ year $_____

Repeat this list of years for questions 17–21.

17. How much did you receive from *member giving* (living donors; exclude endowment income, rents, income from organizations)?

18. How much income did you receive from *church organizations* in each of the years listed?

19. How much income did you receive from *endowments* in each of the years listed?

20. How much income did you receive from *rents and service fees* in each of the years listed?

21. How many giving units (individuals or households who contribute regularly whether they pledge or not) did you have in each of the years listed?

22. Last year, how much did you receive in total from the:
    Ten largest giving units $_____
    Next ten largest giving units $_____

Part V: Program Questions

(On the actual form, leave ample space for responses—10 to 12 lines.)

23. What program or ministry does your unit (do you) do best?

24. What programs or ministries has your unit (have you) initiated or terminated during the past five years?

25. What programs or ministries do you think your unit needs (you need) most to develop during the next five years?

26. What do you see as the two or three most critical issues before this congregation today?

3

A Community Update

The Power of Perception

"You don't know what you're talking about," the older man said. "When you have lived in this neighborhood as long as I did, you will see that what I say is true!"

"Perhaps," the younger man replied, "but I think things really have changed."

I had come to consult with this small middle-city congregation expecting a fairly routine evening. The people were concerned to relate better to the neighborhood immediately around their church building. I had begun by asking members of the church board to describe the neighborhood. That request led rapidly to a hot debate between two board members.

The younger man was a recent arrival to the neighborhood; he and his wife were refurbishing one of the many two-family houses that stretch up and down the streets in that part of the city. He was also a leading force in the revitalization of the church's youth program. Under his guidance, the church had developed a new ministry to some two dozen unchurched young people. Their families, though classified as a "minority group," actually make up a majority of the neighborhood's current residents.

The older man is a native of the church's neighborhood. He was born just after the First World War and grew up during the church's peak years. Until nearly the middle of this century, most of those who walked to work in the old factory at the foot of the hill also walked to attend church services Sundays and the many other activities the church sponsored throughout the week.

Along with most of his childhood friends, the older man was called into military service during the Second World War. Among those fortunate enough to return, he also received benefits under the GI Bill, which enabled him to acquire a college education. After graduation, he went to work for the same corporation, but not as a toolmaker like his father before him. His education enabled him to become an administrator. That higher position also afforded more income, which enabled him to purchase a larger and more expensive house in the suburbs that ring this city.

Through all the changes, his church roots held. He and several other church members, who also live in the suburbs, make regular pilgrimages back to the old city neighborhood to attend church services and church board meetings. They regret many of the changes that have come to their former neighborhood, especially the recent change that has brought new and strange residents, few of whom seem to have any interest in joining, and especially in supporting, the old church. While the older man's statement to the younger man, "When you have lived in the neighborhood as long as I did, you will see . . ." may seem strange to us, it does not seem at all strange to him. He sees the present neighborhood through his memory. Though he has not lived in this neighborhood since he went off to war in 1942, he still believes that it is as he remembers it—or at least it should be.

The younger man sees the neighborhood through his memory as well, though his memory is much shorter and more up-to-date. He has gathered his impressions of the neighborhood over just two years. In his disagreement with the older man, he is simply describing what he sees, most of which the older man has not seen. Therein lies the cause of the argument. Each protagonist is looking at the same neighborhood through different memories. Each of them cannot see what the other sees. And each believes in what he sees.

Each of us has such a personally filtered view of reality. That filter is shaped by what sociologists call our *socialization;* the sum total of all the influences that each of us accept as valid becomes our personal norm of perception. We see the world, or reality, not as it really is but as our norms of perception tell us it is.

Those norms are very powerful. We are usually aware of them only when for some reason we decide they need to be changed. I remember a good friend, now a Roman Catholic bishop, who described one of his old norms during a sermon he preached at the Lutheran church in the neighborhood where he lived as a young boy. His mother had believed Lutherans were dangerous and warned her young son to be wary of them! He confessed to the gathered congregation that during his childhood each time he passed their church he carefully crossed the street to put as much distance as possible between himself and the church building, lest some unforeseen disaster come upon him. Though intellectually he had given up the prejudice long ago, he told them he was surprised that evening to discover he still felt uncomfortable when he walked up the street and approached the Lutheran church building.

Like the bishop, each of us has deeply rooted filters. Even when we decide they are not valid anymore, the feelings around them often linger. That evening as I worked with the city congregation, I was able to help those present to evaluate the accuracy of their varying perceptions of the church's current neighborhood. As the evening progressed, the older man turned out to be quite open to new information, though he confessed that he still wished things were as they had been in the old days.

Whenever your church's leaders make decisions about the church's relationship to its community, they also proceed on the basis of what they think is so. So do you. Those who guide your church need accurate and current information about your community, and especially about the neighborhood in which your church is located. A community update is just as vital to basic planning as a church checkup. Until the younger man challenged them, the leaders in that city congregation were guiding the church on the basis of out-of-date views of the church's neighborhood.

I find such bias surprisingly common among churches. Persons who have long experience with a congregation often move into key leadership posts in that congregation. Some of them hold on to out-of-date perceptions of the church's neighborhood. Leaders who are not aware of important community changes often guide a church away from, rather than toward, an effective relationship to its community. If these leaders influence the minister, they will encourage the minister to move in the same direction. And the minister who follows their guidance will lead the church away from its real potential rather than toward it. Thus a community update, an accurate picture of those factors in the community which are currently affecting your congregation, is critical.

The Community Update Task Force

Just as you chose a task force to complete your church checkup, choose another task force to conduct the community update. If possible, this task force should be composed of different persons and function simultaneously with the checkup task force. Like the checkup, the update is a once-in-every-five-years job. It demands a great deal of effort, but only for a few weeks. While one member of your church's planning committee may serve on this task force to facilitate communication, the majority of the members of the planning committee should save their energy for the planning tasks that will need to be carried out after they receive the task force reports. If your congregation has a limited number of available leaders, appoint a smaller community update task force and extend the work over a longer period of time. If you need to ask some of the same people to serve on both the church checkup and community update groups, you may decide to have the task forces work in succession rather than simultaneously. It is worth taking additional time to do a thorough job of data-gathering.

As you (or whoever has the authority to do so) select persons with the various skills that the task force requires to do its work, you should also attempt to include persons who represent a variety of community experiences and perspectives. Recall the incident that opened this chapter. If your congregation is spread out, it will be helpful to have as members both those who live in the immediate neighborhood where the church building is located and others who live in whatever other neighborhoods from which you draw participants. Seek a balance of women as well as men, older persons as well as younger persons, newer members of your church as well as those who have been members for many years. You yourself should be involved in the work of the task force. The sharpened and up-to-date perceptions the community task force gains will benefit your entire ministry.

You may have among the members of your congregation those whose work naturally recommends them for membership on the community update task force. Those involved professionally as planners, or as members of planning commissions or zoning boards, usually have access to a great deal of data your church will find helpful. Real estate brokers and salespersons are often aware of what types of persons are moving into and out of various neighborhoods. School administrators have up-to-date information about the current and projected number of children of various ages present in your community. They are also aware of those groups with special needs, such as single parents, minorities, and persons with limited capabilities. Those who work with public or private social agencies are excellent sources of information about community needs. Mail carriers and police officers also have helpful firsthand knowledge.

Don't be afraid to invite busy specialists who do not ordinarily work on committees to serve on this task force. You are asking them for a short-term commitment that relates directly to their talents. If you feel they can make a significant contribution, ask them to help.

Gather Data!

Before you and your community update task force begin the work of data-gathering, be certain you understand the difference between information-gathering and data-gathering—and which you seek to do. Some years ago, I served as a member of a committee that approved applications for new church development fields and redevelopment fields in the region where I was a resident. Part of the supporting evidence required for these applications was a self-study that had to be completed by each congregation requesting money. The self-study was quite complex, especially the section entitled Community Analysis. Local leaders had to invest considerable effort assembling comprehensive social and economic information about their communities to complete the applications. Unfortunately, neither they nor we were very clear about the purpose of gathering all that information. But they did the task dutifully, believing that the information they gathered would somehow prove helpful. It rarely did.

I now realize that those churches were gathering *information*, not data. They were given a list of information they needed to find, and they filled in the blanks. Data-gathering is quite different. *Data are items of information gathered for a well-defined and well-understood purpose.* When you go out to collect community data, you know not only what information you need but why you need to gather that information in particular. You are clear that you don't need to know everything about the community, *only what bears on the future of your congregation.*

Perhaps now you understand why I prefer the phrase "community update" to "community analysis." If you know what is presently happening in your church neighborhood that has implications for your congregation, you know what your current options are as a congregation. So long as your church stays where it is, the future of your congregation is bound up with the future of your neighborhood. Note that I did not say "determined by" but "bound up with." I believe your church's best future at its present location will emerge out of the effective interaction of your congregation with the possibilities emerging in your current neighborhood. Those emerging possibilities are key data for you.

Define Your Territory

The first step in beginning your update is to pinpoint your territory. One of the best ways to define the area your congregation serves is to use an old-fashioned pin map. Visit your local city or county planning office and obtain a street map (or, in rural areas, a highway map) that includes as much of the territory your membership covers as possible. Back the map with material that will hold pins securely. Even a large piece of stiff cardboard will do the job, though something like half-inch construction board or bulletin board material will be more permanent. Mark the location of your church building with a suitable symbol. Then place pins at every point on the map where a member of your church lives. While you can use pins of only one color, using several colors to differentiate lengths of membership will enhance the usefulness of your map. As you note the addresses of church families, if you have different-colored pins, note also the date on which they joined the church. Use one color for those who joined within the last three years, another color for those who have joined from three to ten years ago, a third color for those who joined between eleven and twenty years ago, and a fourth color for those who have been members more than twenty years.

When the map is completed, you will be able to *see* whether your church relates to one or several key neighborhoods. If you have used pins of different colors to indicate various lengths of membership, you may discover that the colors tend to cluster. If so, ask yourselves who lives where and why.

Length of membership often coincides with age. Your pin

map may illustrate age concentrations of your congregation. Younger persons are usually not able to afford the more expensive housing that middle-aged persons can.

The map will also show you how local your membership is. If the bulk of your members do not live in the neighborhood immediately around the church, you may discover one reason why you do not have very many members with a natural understanding of what is happening in the church's neighborhood.

I once worked with a smaller congregation in a village located about thirty miles from a major Midwestern city. It was concerned about its lack of growth in the face of a large influx of new residents to the area. The pin map was very revealing. It showed only six of the church's sixty families living within a mile of the church building. The rest were scattered across an area with a twenty-five-mile radius. The church had *no* program aimed at the community; the entire program was aimed inward at the membership. The biggest "problem" (the members all agreed) was trespassing, and on one occasion a break-in, by students from the regional high school that adjoins the church property. They had responded to the break-in by purchasing chains and large locks, which they employed very obviously to secure the building when it was not being used. I tried unsuccessfully to help them see their "problem" as an opportunity. But I found too much animosity to overcome.

Such an extreme reaction is not common. But if you have a significant proportion of members (especially, more than half) who are not local residents, ask yourselves how their attitudes influence the direction your church is taking in its relationship to the immediate neighborhood.

If your church membership is very compact, you may have an opposite problem. Church memberships that come largely from one small neighborhood or settlement often find it difficult to become concerned about the community at large. Small rural congregations, for example, sometimes do not feel much responsibility for problems that affect persons beyond the crossroads where their church building is located. That lack of concern can be just as much of a problem as a city church's lack of concern for its immediate neighborhood, because the entire county may be the functional immediate neighborhood for a rural church.

Of course, your church is not equal to its building. Nevertheless, the location of that building affects your congregation profoundly. The building symbolizes the presence of your congregation in a special way to those who live or work in the area where the building is located. Church members who do not live near the building still feel the effects of the church's neighborhood. If the neighborhood deteriorates, the church building itself may suffer. Special needs of residents in the neighborhood often become a concern of the church, simply because the building is accessible to neighborhood people. Thus, what is likely to happen in the neighborhood around your building holds significant ramifications for the entire congregation, not just for those who happen to live close by.

Informal Research

Only a few of the many profound statements we hear from our teachers stay firmly in our memories. One professor taught me more about research than all the rest combined. And one statement he made during the first hour we spent together has never left me. The course was a tutorial; the subject, guided research. His memorable statement went: "The most sophisticated research instruments you will ever discover are your eyes and your ears. Whenever you begin to do research, look and listen first."

I hope you will profit from his advice as much as I have. Before searching for insights beyond your task force, I suggest you probe the insights *within* your task force. Share what you all see and hear. You may find it helpful to reproduce the work sheet that follows. It suggests that those responding consider changes in population, buildings, institutions, and transportation in the neighborhood around the church. It then provides

space to fill in important changes of the last five years and those
that will occur in the next five years.

WORK SHEET TO DISCOVER POSSIBLE FUTURES
FOR OUR CHURCH*

The purpose of this work sheet is to stimulate your thinking
and help you participate in the vital task of clarifying future
possibilities for our church.

Think about the neighborhood around our church building, especially *population changes,* either growth or decline
(amount), and changes in kinds of persons; *buildings* that
have gone up or structures deteriorated or torn down; *institutions,* what they are and are not doing, and if and how
they are changing (include other churches); *roads* or transportation changes.

1. What important changes have occurred in the neighborhood around our church building in the last five years?

2. What important changes will occur in this neighborhood in the next five years?

---

*In reproducing this work sheet, be sure to provide ample space for
writing responses to the questions.

Make a copy for each member of your task force. After you
have established the key neighborhood(s) to which your church
relates, ask each member to fill it out.

If your experience is typical, the result will be rich and useful
data, especially if you have included persons representing a
variety of neighborhood experiences and involvements on your
task force. The collective wisdom that emerges within the group
will provide up to half the basic data you need to gather about
your neighborhood! Share the insight by asking each member

one by one to talk about his or her responses to the two questions on the work sheet. As each person is talking, write the key ideas on a blackboard or newsprint. Use the first evening to describe what your local experts think has happened and what is likely to happen in your church's neighborhood. Note important issues you all agree are critical. After the meeting, collect the work sheets so you can have someone transcribe the newsprint notes *and* individual responses.

With such a sense of direction, you can continue to assemble useful information simply by walking around your neighborhood or driving through the area. Which of these two strategies you follow next, or whether you do both, depends upon where your church is located. If you are in a city neighborhood, the walk will probably prove more important. The city rarely reveals its true character to those who drive through. I remember my first research in a ghetto neighborhood, guided by someone with a sensitive, experienced eye. The neighborhood looked very shabby to me—all of it, to begin with! But my guide, an Episcopal priest, began to point out what my outsider's eyes did not see. This family (he pointed to a partly hidden plot of ground) had begun a garden in only a few feet of space; what lovely tomato plants! Few of the houses on another block were owned by their occupants; you could tell, he noted, because they were in poor repair. On yet another street the houses looked much better; more of them were owned by the residents. There the neighborhood organization was strong; they had pressed the city to turn a vacant lot into a playground. Look caringly as you go!

When you walk through the neighborhood, ask one or more residents to guide you. Listen to what their eyes see. Ask questions like, "Who is on the street at ten in the morning, at noon, at four, at eight, at midnight?" Even the number of people on the street is significant, indicating as it does whether people in the neighborhood feel relatively safe to be outdoors. Think not only in terms of children but, in the summer months especially, of the number of older people walking or sitting on their front steps. To gain a complete picture of neighborhood life, you may need to take strolls at different times of day.

As you walk around, ask those you meet how they feel about the neighborhood. What do they like about it? What are the problems they see? You may be pleasantly surprised how talkative people will be—and how much you will learn.

Then take a drive around all the other neighborhoods, through the entire area your church serves. If you can, ask residents to guide you. As you proceed, ask yourselves questions about what you see. In which neighborhoods are there bicycles in the yards? Where do children play in the street? Where they do, is it because they have no place else to play? Is there a gang hanging around the candy store or the convenience food store?

Where do neighborhood transitions occur? What happens when you cross the interstate or go under the railroad tracks? Think of the pin map of your church families. Is your congregation equally accessible from the viewpoint of those who live in all the neighborhoods you visit? Look at your church through the eyes of various persons who might be active in your church.

Are changes in your area affecting your congregation's visibility? For example, have there been any significant shifts in the major flow of traffic recently? Those shifts can have profound effects. Not long ago, I was asked by a regional judicatory to work with one of their congregations located in what they said was "the middle of" a suburban area. The suburb was growing rapidly, the church not at all. The church's leaders told me they also wanted the congregation to grow but couldn't seem to attract anyone. They were puzzled at the lack of growth. Nearly all the leaders live within an old village, now surrounded by suburban developments. The church is located on what the leaders believe is actually, as well as in name, Main Street. "We're at the center of things," they told me. "The church is right at the hub."

"How are the stores doing in the village?" I asked. "Not too well," they responded. That made me suspicious. The next day I drove around with two of them. Most new housing is located between the old village and the interstate. In the midst of the housing developments is a rapidly growing church of a similar denomination, established as a new church development field when the housing began. Near the interstate exit there is a new shopping center, busy most of the time. Few of those who live in the new housing have any reason to travel to "the center of things," the old village Main Street. Most of them are employed in the suburban ring and travel to their place of work on the interstate. They can do their shopping at the shopping center, also in the opposite direction from the church.

The leaders had been expecting the congregation to grow naturally as it had for several generations. They found their church attractive and convenient. They had not seen it through the eyes of newer residents, for whom it was clearly not "at the center of things."

More Formal Approaches

Over the years, I have found that many congregations gain all the community data they need to begin basic planning using only informal approaches to data-gathering. Especially in congregations for whom informal planning is most natural, such informal approaches to data-gathering feel more satisfactory than the formal research upon which many of us have learned to depend.

The ultimate goal of church planning is not to gather data but to move a congregation toward more effective ministry and mission. If your community update task force gathers sufficient data through informal approaches to challenge your congregation adequately for several years, and the typical mode of planning in your congregation will encourage sufficient response to such informal research, please do not feel you need to go on to complete the formal research procedures outlined in this section. In fact, if yours is a smaller congregation, you may discover that data gathered through formal research, especially research carried on by nonmembers, will have less credibility and be less likely to lead to action on the part of the congregation than data gathered by trusted local leaders following sound, informal approaches.

All these observations are not meant to discount the importance of solid, formal research. There are many situations that demand a more systematic approach because "hard" data are required to provide an adequate base for planning. Sometimes leaders look around them and still don't see what needs to be done. Consider the case of a congregation located on the edge of a Southern city. Data assembled informally by its planning committee indicated that single parents lived in the neighborhood around the church building. Committee members spoke with several church members who were residents of the neighborhood. Each of them knew of a few homes where only one parent was present. There was some talk in the church board of the possibility of setting up a day-care center to meet the neighborhood's needs. But most of the board members at the time were not residents of the immediate neighborhood and were less than enthusiastic about the proposal. To justify their case to the board, the planning committee members felt they needed more solid data, which by their definition meant hard, factual data. I suggested they check with the neighborhood elementary school, on the assumption that the school would have a record of parents of children enrolled and thus would have tabulated the number of single parents. The school did have such a record and the proportion turned out to be a staggering two thirds of the households. On the basis of such solid evidence, the planning committee went on to prepare a proposal for the day-care center, which the church board then approved.

This congregation made another unexpected discovery when its planning committee members called the school. The information they needed was there for the asking. Someone else had already done the work. Most church leaders are quite surprised to learn how much help is available simply for the asking. Many clergy function independently, believing the model pastor is one who can solve all problems that come along. Such pastors rarely encourage lay leaders in their congregation to seek help from outside sources.

Doing the work yourselves will waste a goodly amount of energy if others have already done it. If you and your task force need data about your neighborhood or community beyond what you can gather by informal means, I suggest you consult the other professionals *before* you begin what is usually a long process of data-gathering and analysis. The Community Interviews work sheet may prove helpful. City and county planning offices, social agencies, police and fire departments, the U.S. Department of Agriculture Extension Service, university planning departments, state planning departments, local and state councils of churches, and many others usually have collected and analyzed data that will answer your needs. Beyond the fact of having the data available, such organizations are already familiar with them. They can often guide you to precise pages that answer your questions, or show you key tables and graphs. And usually everything they do is free! In fact, most of them are supposed to be helpful to the public, especially to other organizations that benefit the public good. When they help you, they are doing their jobs in the process.

The largest single source of community data in most areas is the U.S. census of population and housing. If you need to gather formal demographic data for your community, you will probably turn to this source. If you or others in your task force are not familiar with census data, seek guidance from those who are.

There are many who can help you. Most of the data with which public agencies work is drawn from current and past U.S. censuses. To facilitate their use of the census, state-level planning agencies, most state universities, and many county and city groups purchase computer tapes of census data for the areas within their jurisdiction. A major advantage of data filed electronically is the ease of access. You can request, and the computer will supply only what you need. Usually you can have the data in either table form or computer-produced graphs or both.

And the small cost may surprise you. Generally, you will be able to purchase everything you need for $100 or less. Or it will be free, a service of the agency you consult.

What census data are most likely to be helpful to update your

COMMUNITY INTERVIEWS

Types of persons to interview:

- Those who deal professionally with the community, such as the mayor, police chief, sheriff, and school administrators, agriculture extension agents, Chamber of Commerce executives, business and labor leaders, other ministers.
- Those who live and/or work in the community, such as storekeepers, schoolteachers, filling station attendants, homemakers.
- Those who might hold a special point of view, such as teenagers, elderly persons, landlords, tenants, minority persons.

Some questions it may be helpful to ask*:

1. What important trends or changes do you see happening in our community in the next five years?

2. What do you feel are the major unmet needs of our community?

3. What kinds of persons need help and aren't finding it?

4. What do you think the _____ church could do to be helpful in our community?

---

*Add questions specifically related to current programs or ministries your church carries out or is contemplating.

congregation to the challenges of ministry and mission in your area? Some of the more valuable items I usually examine are: (1) various characteristics of the population, including age, marital status, average number of persons per household, single-parent households as a percent of all households, median school years completed, percent of high school graduates, percent who changed residence within the past five years, occupational characteristics, median income, percent of families with income below poverty level; and (2) housing characteristics, such as median number of rooms, median value of housing, median rent.

The data you can obtain are determined by what is available for your type of area. The smallest unit for which the census has data available is the city block. Block data are quite limited and available only within areas that are "tracted." Much more data are available at the tract level. Census tracts are defined by the bureau within major metropolitan areas designated as Standard Metropolitan Statistical Areas (SMSA). In its description, the census bureau states that

> tracts were generally designed to be relatively uniform with respect to population characteristics, economic status, and living conditions. The average tract has about 4,000 residents. Tract boundaries are established with the intention of being maintained over a long time so that comparisons may be made from census to census.

To honor the maintenance of tract boundaries, the bureau may subdivide tracts as population grows and add new tracts as metropolitan areas expand, but rarely does it change the boundaries of existing tracts.

Areas that lie outside Standard Metropolitan Statistical Areas are not tracted. Here I find much of the data I need for church planning available at the county level and for what the bureau terms Minor Civil Divisions (MCDs), which include townships, towns, and villages.

Some census data are available according to zip codes. If the data you need are available at this level, and you can sort your congregation by zip codes, you may gain important insights by comparing your church members who live in a specific zip code with the total population of that zip code.

The best approach is to decide what you need to know and then look for data at the level that matches the focus of your inquiry. I suggest you visit your local library or planning office to identify the census unit or units that relate to your church. If your church is in a nonmetropolitan area, you will find data filed according to your MCD both in written reports and on computer tape. If your congregation's building is located within a tracted area, examine a tract map for your SMSA. Locate your church on the tract map. Record the tract number within which it lies. You may discover you need to include more than one tract to encompass your congregation's area of influence. Note the numbers of all the tracts, if that is the case. Consult written reports or request computer output in relation to the items you are concerned about for all the tracts included within your church's neighborhood or area of influence.

Exactly what you ask for depends, of course, on the purpose you need the data to serve. For example, if you want to find out what new ministries are needed in your community, you may want to study items like percent of persons over the age of 62, number of children under the age of 18, percent of those aged 16 to 21 years not high school graduates and not enrolled in school, percent of families headed by a single parent, percent of families with income below poverty level, and so forth.

If you want to discover possible sources of new members or increased support for your church, you may want to identify tracts where population has increased, or tracts with high average family size, or tracts with a large number of persons present of the type to whom you hope to appeal. Or you may want to know the median income of families within the area your church serves in order to determine whether your hoped-for level of support is realistic, especially if your church is considering increasing its budget significantly.

As you work, don't forget that data can be obtained in graphs as well as tables. When you ask for data in graph form, it is easy visually to compare similar data for your church and neighborhood by drawing a graph for your congregation on the same scale as the census graph and laying it on top of the graph produced from census data. Simply run them both through a copier that makes overhead transparencies. We will explore these comparative possibilities more fully in Chapter 4. The census is rich in data. It can be extremely useful, when you are clear about what you need and how you will use it.

Designing Your Own Survey

Sometimes a task force does informal research and searches census data and other available sources and still faces important unanswered questions. For example, your research may lead you to think there are persons in your area who represent possible members for your church, but you aren't sure. Or you may believe there are residents in your church's neighborhood who need ministry from your congregation, but you want to describe their needs more clearly. In either case, you need to identify *and* contact particular persons to discover if and how they will relate to your church. Such data are generally not obtainable from the census or other usual community sources, simply because such sources do not gather religious preference data or any other data designed specifically to be used by churches.

Typically, congregations carry out surveys to assess ministry needs or growth potential both cooperatively and individually. For instance, churches in a rapidly growing community or one that is undergoing radical change may join together to survey their area. Such cooperative surveys are usually designed to discover those individuals not related to any church and which of various congregations, if any, such persons might prefer. Instruments designed to be used in these surveys are readily available from councils of churches and denominational evangelism offices.

If you decide to recommend cooperation with a group that

utilizes a prepared questionnaire, examine the instrument carefully to be certain the joint effort will provide the specific data you need as a church.

The best approach is to survey your area yourselves. Even if an individual approach means you cover less ground, I still recommend it. You have a much better chance of gaining the data that relate specifically to your congregation. You can decide what you need to know and shape a questionnaire that guides interviewers to gather the information you need.

There is another advantage that may not be obvious at first sight. Someone who is clearly identified as from your congregation will visit the households of those persons who either represent potential members for your church or need the ministry of your congregation. That personal contact, in my opinion, is as important as gathering data—in fact, in the long run it may be even more important. A well-designed and well-executed neighborhood survey should not only yield good data, it should also build relationships between your church and those you want to contact. If you choose to suggest such a survey to your planning committee, be sure to point out this relationship-building potential.

The Community Survey Questionnaire at the end of the chapter is an instrument you can employ if you decide you want to recommend a survey to locate possible members for your congregation. The suggested questions will help visitors discover which of those they interview are currently participating in a congregation, to what extent the interviewee is familiar with your congregation, and, if so, how he or she feels about your congregation. Other questions test possible interest respondents may have in specific church programs, their basic level of interest in your church, and, finally, some demographic questions. After the interviewer departs, the instrument suggests that he or she add personal impressions and any recommendations for follow-up.

A well-done community update can be extremely helpful to your church planning committee and your congregation. It can uncover new possibilities for ministry and growth that challenge and revitalize your congregation. It can help your congregation be the church of Jesus Christ relevantly and currently in your neighborhood.

Specific suggestions that your community update task force can follow as they prepare their report to the planning committee are similar to those offered to the church checkup task force at the end of Chapter 2. Whoever guides the community update task force in summarizing its report can consult these suggestions for guidance.

COMMUNITY SURVEY QUESTIONNAIRE

Opening. I'm from ——— Church. We are taking a survey in this area to discover how we can better serve the needs of those who live here. You can help us discover how to serve by answering a few questions.

1. Are you currently participating in a church?
   ——— Yes
   ——— No (If no, go to No. 4.)

2. What is the name of that church?

   _____

3. If you attend worship services, how often do you do this?
   ——— Every week
   ——— 2 or 3 times a month
   ——— Once a month
   ——— Only on special occasions

4. If you do not now participate, did you ever attend a church?
   ——— Yes
   ——— No (If no, go to No. 6.)

5. When and what church did you attend?

   _____

   How long ago did you last attend regularly? ———years

6. Do other *adults* in your household currently participate in a church?
    _____ Yes
    _____ No (If no, go to No. 8.)

7. In which church(es) do they participate?_____

8. Do *children* or *teenagers* in your household participate in a church?
    _____ Yes
    _____ No (If no, go to No. 10.)

9. In which church(es) do they participate?_____

10. How familiar are you with those who attend ——— Church?
    _____ Very familiar
    _____ Quite familiar
    _____ A little familiar
    _____ Not familiar

11. How do you feel about the idea of attending ——— Church?
    _____ Very comfortable
    _____ Quite comfortable
    _____ A little comfortable
    _____ Uncomfortable

12. Why do you feel this way?_____

13. If you were to attend ——— Church, in which of the following might you participate?
    _____ Worship service
    _____ Sunday school
    _____ Youth group*

*List all groups that now function in your church or that you are considering. Larger churches with complex programs may wish to print a separate card to hand to the respondent to check. Be sure to attach card securely to questionnaire when respondent hands it back.

14. If you were able to find a church exactly as you wanted it to be, what would that church be like?

15. What is your current level of interest in ——— Church?
    _____ Would like to participate
    _____ Would like someone to visit with more information
    _____ Would like to be on the mailing list

16. How many persons in your household are in each age group?
    _____ 0–4 _____ 10–14 _____ 20–34 _____ 50–64
    _____ 5–9 _____ 15–19 _____ 35–49 _____ 65+

17. What is your occupation?_____

    Occupation(s) of others who live here?_____

18. In what community groups are you (and others in this household) active?_____

19. What was the last year of school each person who lives here completed?
    _____ Adult 1   Adult 3_____   Child 2_____
    _____ Adult 2   Child 1_____   Child 3_____

20. If you think you might like more information about our church in the future, may I have your name and address?
    Name_____
    Address_____

Thank interviewee.
After you leave, write in address, even if interviewee did not give it to you. Add your own personal impressions and suggestions for follow-up.

4

Making Plans

Plans are made, not born. When working with a group of church leaders, rarely have I been inspired to produce a fully developed action plan. Most pastors I know have a similar experience. So if you and your church leaders struggle through the data you gather to decide which are the most significant issues you must address and then spend more long nights shaping those issues into well-developed action plans, pause occasionally along the way and take some comfort from the fact that your experience is normal. Like the rest of us, you have to "make" your plans.

If in your church checkup and community update task forces you have followed the guidelines suggested in this book, however, your work should be easier. Those task forces will have furnished you with clearly described issues and solid support data that clarify why these issues are significant for your church to address during the next five years. With the receipt of their reports, the major work of your planning committee begins.

Bring It All Together

Conclude the data-gathering process in your congregation with a conference attended by members of both task forces and your planning committee. This does not mean that you should hold such a conference in place of asking each task force for a written report. The discipline of a written report from each task force will give your planning committee the benefit of their critical thinking, especially if you ask them to follow the format suggested at the end of Chapter 2. Circulating these written reports to members of the task forces and planning committee *before* the conference will help everyone prepare to participate more effectively. It also means that participants will not need to spend as much time during the meeting assimilating the *content* of the task force reports. You can use the conference for clarification, discussion, critical reflection, and listening to the feelings that task force members have about the data they have gathered and the issues they have identified.

How complex and lengthy your data-gathering conference needs to be depends on the complexity of the issues that emerge from your task forces. If the issues are fairly routine and refer easily to existing groups or individuals, you may even be able to complete the summary in an evening. In my experience, however, an evening is rarely sufficient. Processing the information generally requires a block of time of at least five or six hours *in meetings,* with added time for breaks and a meal. That expands the event itself to seven and one-half or eight hours—which means either a morning plus an afternoon or an afternoon plus an evening. The issues of basic planning are too important to slight by rushing through the data-gathering conference. If you give the hard work of your task force inadequate consideration, everyone loses.

Therefore, you might think in terms of an all-day Saturday conference, or one running through Sunday afternoon into the evening, as a minimum. If you are able to go away somewhere as a group for an overnight beginning with Friday supper, for example, and running through Saturday midafternoon, you will find the extra time spent very worthwhile.

Whatever time frame you choose for your conference, there are some helpful steps that your planning committee can take in preparation. Each member should read through the reports of your task forces carefully. As you work your way through each task force's data, ask yourselves whether you come to the same conclusions as they do. Then meet together to identify key issues that challenge your congregation. It will probably help to begin with summary questions.

1. Is our church growing? If it is, what are the implications of that growth for us? If it is not, what are the implications of that lack of growth? Given our location, can we expect to grow? Does our congregation want to grow? What types of persons can we look to as the sources of our growth? How might we appeal to them?

2. What implications stem from the age distribution of our congregation? Do we have a dominant age group? If so, what does the dominance of this group mean for us? Are there age groups for whom we do not program adequately? Are there any we do not include within the leadership and decision-making of our congregation?

3. What does the sex ratio of our congregation tell us? How well do we address the particular needs of women? Of men?

4. Are there types of households or families for whom we do not provide adequate program or ministry? What about single adults and single parents? Older middle-aged husbands and wives who no longer have children at home?

5. Are our facilities adequate? More than adequate? Do we have more building than we can support? Do we face major building expenses, or need to make major changes, or even construct new facilities during the next five years?

6. Are we keeping up financially? If we aren't, why aren't we? Do we depend too much on a few people or one source of income? Have we failed to recognize the loss of one kind of income (for example, from a church organization)? Have we failed to develop a significant source of income (for example, rentals, endowments)?

7. What are the most important issues identified by our church organizations?

8. What key changes are occurring with the neighborhood(s) or community with which our church interacts? Are

groups emerging that challenge us (younger adults, minorities)? Is our congregation more like or less like the community than it was ten years ago? Five years ago? Is the leadership of our congregation representative of those who currently live in the area around the church building? Are our church leaders aware of what is happening in the neighborhood around our church building?

Committee members will very likely raise their own questions. Suggest that each record key points (especially any disagreements) to talk over at the conference.

At the conference itself, spend the first half of the meeting clarifying major issues. Note especially those issues which the planning committee identified in their consideration of the task force reports, including any challenges they wish to offer. Move quickly through issues everyone understands so that you have enough time to clarify those about which there is some confusion.

If your group is small (less than twelve), you can probably work as a single group. If your group is larger than twelve, I suggest you subdivide. If you do subdivide, be sure to include representatives from *each* task force *and* the planning committee within each subgroup. Also, you will need to allow time to regather and share the results of the subgroup discussions.

Conclude the initial discussion by prioritizing the issues you have clarified. To do so, simply list on separate pieces of newsprint by four categories. Place the appropriate heading at the top of each piece of newsprint to indicate the priority of those issues a majority believe should fall into that category. The categories are:

1. High priority: *must do* during the next five years.
2. Medium priority: *should do* during the next five years.
3. Low priority: *optional to do* during the next five years.
4. Unclear priority: *can't agree* about priority for the next five years.

If you use a daylong format, it will probably be helpful to have a break before you prioritize the issues. If you use an overnight format, I suggest you spend the evening clarifying the issues and begin the following morning by prioritizing.

Suppose you have difficulty agreeing about the priority of some issues. If fewer than three quarters of those present in a group agree about the priority of an issue, attempt to identify the reasons for disagreement (insufficient data, too expensive, serves the needs of too few, value or theological disagreements —which we shall see require special attention). List the reasons along with the issues under category 4, Unclear priority, for referral back to the planning committee. Do *not* become involved in a lengthy discussion of one or two issues. It is sufficient at this stage to list issues about which there is disagreement and then move on to clarify and prioritize the rest.

During the last block of time at the data-gathering conference, discuss ways your congregation might implement at least those issues you agree have high priority and, if there is time, those issues you think have medium priority. If you subdivide for this new discussion period, list similar issues together on newsprint and assign them to the same subgroup. As you consider referrals for action to individuals, groups, and organizations, be sure you are aware of their current work loads. Try to assess realistically whether the individuals or groups can carry out the work you envision for them.

Finally, meet together to share the results of your work and to define at least one overall issue (but no more than three issues) to challenge your congregation for the next five years. What consuming concern(s) will engage you together as God's people for that time period?

Although you may not follow the precise format suggested here to conclude your data-gathering process, it is important to set aside enough time together to summarize and agree about the issues that will challenge your congregation for the next five years. Your planning committee needs to gain an accurate picture of what the task forces found; the task forces need to feel satisfied that the planning committee has heard them accurately and appreciates the work they have done. Whether that process takes you one meeting or several, do it well.

Seek a Mandate

After your planning committee has received the issues from the two task forces through either a data-gathering conference or another means of your own design, you then need to move on to prepare proposals for approval by the appropriate church board(s). It seems futile to do the hard work of preparing detailed action plans only to discover that your church boards do not agree that your hard work should be implemented. It makes far more sense to state key issues clearly, prepare brief proposals for dealing with each, and gain approval for the proposals first.

If you have chosen persons who are truly representative of your congregation and its leaders to serve as members of your planning committee and task forces, they will provide reliable guidance about the acceptability and priority of the issues you clarify. As you review the suggestions stemming from the data-gathering conference, you need only clarify and be certain the supporting evidence is adequate for those about which your planning committee and task forces have consensus.

Those proposals about which you do *not* have consensus call for more extensive consideration. Issues about which you disagree in the committee will not be likely to receive endorsement by the appropriate board as proposals for action unless you are able to be clear about the nature of your disagreement and then, if you still choose to recommend a proposal for action, why you have decided to do so.

You need not have *total* agreement in your planning committee about every proposal you recommend for action. In fact, you probably will not have unanimous support for everything you suggest. But you do need to know whose interest or needs each suggestion will serve. This awareness is especially important if your congregation is dominated by one group that sets the tone and direction of its life, or if you have subgroups with conflicting values.

If your planning committee emerged from the data-gathering process with issues about which you disagree, try to move below the surface of the disagreement. Do you have a dominant group in your congregation? Or do several groups vie for dominance? If so, seek to move your congregation toward more openness and inclusiveness in your proposals to the church board(s). As your planning committee presents its proposals, you may need to explain that some proposals are included not because they seem critical to every member of the committee but because they are designed to stretch the church's ministry, reaching into the lives of others in your church or area not now adequately included or recognized within the church's current ministries.

A representative planning group distinct from the policy board(s) sometimes has the detachment and capacity to help a church come to terms with the implications of inhibiting factions. Such a group can show how disagreements over priorities indicate that the congregation should broaden its purposes to include the needs and concerns of groups beyond a dominant core group, or to recognize the priorities of different groups as equally legitimate. Church growth, whether in numbers or in depth, is really a matter of church change. A church grows as it changes. A church that does not change rarely grows. Basic church planning gives you an opportunity to define proposals that will challenge your church to widen its ministry.

Prepare each proposal you wish to recommend to your church board as a brief statement of action to be taken, then point out why the church needs to act at this time. State whether the proposal is to be referred to an existing group or individual for development into an action plan, or whether you intend to develop it yourselves as a planning committee, perhaps by assembling a task force.

In addition to a suggested course of implementation, you will help the board make a decision if you also include with your proposals an assessment of their individual and cumulative impact on the present organization, resource allocation, and staff of your congregation. Generally speaking, the more your proposals fall within the bounds of existing organizational groups, the less change they imply for the church as a whole; the more general they are, the more change they will demand, and the more they may threaten existing groups or persons.

Church organization usually lags behind change; it lags both in total amount and in focus. Churches that are declining tend to have too much organization. As is usually the case with the church building, their organizational structure is often suitable for a congregation much larger than they now have. On the other hand, churches that are growing rapidly often have too little organization. In one congregation for whom I worked, for example, the Christian education committee chairperson has always served as the Sunday school superintendent. When the church was small, the role was quite manageable; but now, with over 250 in the Sunday school, the organization needs to be expanded to provide for two offices and two persons. So the first question is, Do you need to suggest a scaling up or a scaling down organizationally?

Then there is the matter of the *focus* of your organization, and your budget and staff as well. You may wish to point out that some of your proposals challenge the existing allocation of resources because in your analysis some resources should be reallocated to move your church toward different challenges. I find that churches often maintain programs in line with traditional directions long after the need for them has vanished, or at least has been greatly reduced. If your data point toward a change in focus with an accompanying reallocation of organization, resources, and staff, be bold in your recommendations and clear about your reasons for suggesting the changes.

In summary, we can outline the steps of basic planning in a simple diagram, as seven steps.

BASIC PLANNING PROCESS

Step 1: Data-gathering by task forces
  Step 2: Conference with planning committee
    Step 3: Preparing proposals
      Step 4: Approval by policy board(s)
        Step 5: Preparing action plan
          Step 6: Approval by policy board(s)
          Step 7: Implementation

Once your proposals have gained approval from the appropriate policy board(s) (step 4), you are ready to move on to action planning (step 5).

Plan Action That Happens

Most planning, even when proposals have been approved, does not lead to action. Usually, this is because the objectives are not clear and/or the plans are not specific. If you and your committee follow the suggestions in this section, you should be able to avoid both pitfalls.

Unfortunately, most local church leaders try to implement ideas, not objectives. Even an idea that seems clear and for which you have solid support can be difficult to translate into an action plan. To illustrate, suppose your planning committee and church checkup task force agree that your church needs to reach out to young adults moving into your area. Everybody seems clear about what is to happen: they want the church to reach the younger adults. But as clear as the idea seems, it is still difficult to say exactly what it means and to decide how to go about moving from the idea to action.

The idea needs refining. An idea is the raw material of planning; it is something that might be, or could happen. To build an action plan, an idea needs to be refined into an objective, or *something specific to be achieved by a certain person or group within a definite period of time.*

Imagine how your planning committee might go about refining the idea of reaching young adults To begin with, what do you know *specifically* about those you want to reach? Suppose your research data shows that those younger adults who are new to your community, whether male or female, tend to be employed full-time outside their homes, tend to be childless, well educated, and so on. With good data, you can translate your idea into an objective that states *in specific terms* what you hope to achieve. For example, you might propose: "By November 15, our church will bring together three dialogue groups focused on issues of concern to the participants; each group will be composed of 12 to 15 younger adults who have moved to our area within the last three years and who are not now active in any church." That objective is *specific, achievable,* and *measurable.* Reading it, you know when your church plans to achieve the objective (by November 15), you know exactly what you want to achieve (groups of specifically described new persons who identify issues they want to address), and the standard by which the achievement will be measured (three groups of 12 to 15 persons each). The objective lends itself much more clearly to the development of an action plan than the original plan.

Any objective you develop should state clearly what you intend to achieve, when you intend to achieve it, and what standard will determine whether you have achieved it. Restate your ideas or proposals as objectives. You may have to rewrite several times.

Once you have a clear objective, you are ready to move toward an action plan. List all the steps you need to take to implement each objective. Don't be concerned about the order, just list them. In a group setting, I find it most helpful to write them on newsprint or a blackboard. Continuing with the illustration, action steps such as these might emerge:

- Understand the spiritual development needs of younger adults like those new to our community.
- Find out where they live.

- Discover what meeting times are best for them.
- Learn how to lead, or find a leader suitable for a dialogue group that would interest them.
- Get out the news about the group we intend to begin to those who might respond.

Once you have listed all the action steps, arrange them sequentially. Which steps have to be completed before which other steps? For example, research like "Find out where they live" has to precede "Discover what meeting times are best for them."

After you order the steps, work out the details of each step. Let's suppose "Understand the spiritual development needs of younger adults like those new to our community" is the first action step your planning committee decides to take. The Action Planner that follows gives the elements that compose an action step: the time needed, the resources needed, the target date, and the person responsible. Whenever you define those elements clearly, action is more likely to occur. In putting the above action step on the first line of your Action Planner, you might estimate three persons will be needed to gather and review the information. Purchasing or renting the materials will cost about $75. Reading and reviewing will consume 45 hours. The task will take two weeks. And Mary Smith is willing to see that it is completed.

Even if some of your estimates are not accurate, the fact that you have defined in detail what needs to be accomplished raises the possibility that the action step will happen. You have counted the cost in persons and time as well as dollars. When you write people's names into the action steps, you need to ask them whether they will do what you have defined. By listing a target date, you bring some urgency to the task. And by listing someone as responsible, *and always only one,* you identify clearly who is accountable to see that this action step happens.

I always recommend using a format for action planning similar to this one. Filling out a form with required information may

ACTION PLANNER

OBJECTIVE _____

CHAIRPERSON _____ TARGET DATE _____

Step Number and Description (When parallel, use letters also: 2a, 2b, etc.)	Resources Needed (Persons, dollars, items)	Time Needed (hours)	Target Date	Person Responsible (One name only)

seem overly tedious, but it has some real advantages. It may save you from imagining you have designed something, when all you have really done is think about it. Completing the form also helps those who are not naturally designers to become designers. Many (most?) people have real difficulty defining and holding together all the elements that need to be included to complete an action plan. When you and your committee follow a format, it is much easier for everyone to see what needs to be done and then work together to complete the plan.

You know your plan is finished when you have completed all the action steps. You also will discover whether your plan, as your first conceived it, is realistic in terms of time and resources. If your experience is similar to most churches, when you actually complete an action plan you will often find you must allow more time and/or resources than you had originally envisioned.

Once your planning committee has agreed about a planning format, whether it is mine or another better suited to your needs, I suggest you ask all groups in your congregation to use the same format. If you write the names of the people accountable on each action plan, you will see easily whether some church leaders are involved in more than is healthy, either for them or for the congregation.

Using the same format makes it easier to share with one another what you are seeking to accomplish. It also enables you to see the total resources you are going to need to complete all the action plans. If you have been specific, when you lay all the action plans side by side you will be able to see quickly whether the total demands to be placed on the church's resources are reasonable. And you will be able to see the overall direction basic planning lays out for your church over the next several years.

Basic planning is similar to calculating the trajectory for a space vehicle. If the calculations for that trajectory are based on accurate data, a well-launched vehicle will proceed where those who launch it want it to go. Mostly. Unforeseen circumstances will arise. These necessitate "mid-course corrections." The systems of the vehicle need to be monitored en route, and adjustments made. But all these actions, like annual planning in a church, are designed to keep the vehicle headed on its original course. They occur within the original flight plan.

You can follow the same format for annual planning with each church organization and committee as you employed to complete your basic planning. Such routine plans usually involve the same steps and are generally carried on according to the same time line. Once you do an action plan for such recurring tasks as building a budget or recruiting teachers, you can follow it year after year simply by making new persons responsible for the various action steps listed.

Whenever your annual planning reveals a number of overall issues that seriously challenge the basic direction and organization of your congregation, you will probably need to undertake basic planning again. If such is the case, all the excitement and challenge of setting new directions await you, your planning committee, and your congregation.

Index